The Intelligent Divorce
Because Your Kids Come First

Book Two:
Taking Care of Yourself

Advance Praise

"Dr. Banschick's unique and credible voice is pragmatic and optimistic. The anecdotal evidence throughout the book rings true, and this makes *The Intelligent Divorce* an important read."

—RICHARD FRANCIS, M.D.
CLINICAL TEXTBOOK OF ADDICTION DISORDERS
FOUNDING PRESIDENT, AMERICAN ACADEMY OF ADDICTION PSYCHIATRY

"*The Intelligent Divorce* is a blessing. It ought to become required reading for any professional in the mental health or legal field. The book's incredible thoughtfulness and common sense invites practitioners to offer alternative, cooperative approaches, especially when children are involved."

—SAM KLAGSBRUN, M.D.
CEO, FOUR WINDS HOSPITAL SYSTEM
CHAIRMAN OF PASTORAL COUNSELING, JEWISH THEOLOGICAL SEMINARY

"It isn't merely a book; it's a tool that anyone going through a divorce should be required to implement. It belongs on the desk of all divorce lawyers, judges, child psychologists, and every divorced or divorcing parent."

—CATHY MEYER
CERTIFIED DIVORCE CONSULTANT,
FOUNDER, DIVORCEDWOMENONLINE.COM

"Dr. Banschick's encyclopedic book on divorce can be of inestimable value to anyone considering or already in the process of a divorce."

—LOUIS GETOFF, PH.D.
INSTITUTE OF IMAGO RELATIONSHIP THERAPY
CLINICAL PSYCHOLOGIST AND PSYCHOANALYST

"Comprehensive, well organized, and user friendly, *The Intelligent Divorce* is a must read for any professional caring for children."

—PETER ACKER, MD, FAAP, CHAIRMAN,
DEPT. OF PEDIATRICS, GREENWICH HOSPITAL

"Dr. Banschick is a rare talent, as practical as Dr. Phil, as soulful as Rabbi Kushner and as savvy about men and woman as John Gray. He can guide rebuilding families so that they not only survive, but thrive."

—JILL BROOKE
CONTRIBUTOR, HUFFINGTON POST

"The Intelligent Divorce" covers everything a parent needs to provide for their children in an emotionally healthy manner. This is a very powerful book that should be read by anyone providing care for children of divorce."

—LINDA RANSON JACOBS
DIRECTOR, SINGLE PARENTING DIVISION, NATIONAL CENTER
FOR BIBLICAL PARENTING
AUTHOR, CHURCH INITIATIVE'S DIVORCECARE FOR KIDS
WWW.DC4K.ORG AND THE PARENTZONE

"*The Intelligent Divorce* is of critical importance for divorcing couples. Following his masterful presentation at our family institute in Jerusalem we adopted his program for divorcing couples in our community, and it has made a significant difference. I strongly recommend this book."

—YISRAEL LEVITZ, PH.D.
DIRECTOR, FAMILY INSTITUTE OF NEVE YERUSHALAYIM, ISRAEL
CLINICAL PSYCHOLOGIST, PROFESSOR EMERITUS, YESHIVA UNIVERSITY

"Dr. Banschick brings the message of a healthier divorce to parents and professionals who need to hear it. His program serves as a virtual classroom in how to handle one of life's toughest problems."

—LEONARD SHYLES, PH.D.
ASSOCIATE PROFESSOR OF COMMUNICATIONS, VILLANOVA UNIVERSITY

"*The Intelligent Divorce* is a gem. It's reader friendly and engaging and provides quality guidance on what to do, not just what not to do."

—ROBERT ROCCO COTTONE, PH.D., PROFESSOR OF COUNSELING
AND FAMILY THERAPY, UNIVERSITY OF MISSOURI-SAINT LOUIS,
AUTHOR, *TOWARD A POSITIVE PSYCHOLOGY OF
RELIGION: BELIEF SCIENCE IN THE MODERN ERA*

"*The Intelligent Divorce* provides a wise and comforting voice of understanding and wisdom for easing the pain surrounding divorce. I highly recommend this book."

—Rabbi David Ellenson, President
Hebrew Union College-Jewish Institute of Religion

"Finally a book that focuses on raising healthy, resilient children when divorce is part of their growing up experience. By writing a practical, comprehensive book, designed not to make parents feel guilty about their decision to separate and divorce, but rather designed to help parents make good decisions while they co-parent during and after the divorce, Dr. Banschick is contributing to the well being of the next generation."

—Rita S. Pollak
Partner Pollak Heenan Collaborative Enterprises
Past-President, International Association
of Collaborative Professionals

"*The Intelligent Divorce: Taking Care of Yourself* delivers an equally powerful punch as did Book One: *Taking Care of Your Children.* Dr. Banschick highlights the importance of learning not to let your ex get to you while showing you how to cope with anger, anxiety, and unhealthy parenting practices. The book presents practical spirituality, a financial primer for single parents, and action plans for taking control of your fate. I cannot stress enough how beneficial Dr. Banschick's *Intelligent Divorce* series is to those we say we love the most but continually fight over and about: our children."

—Michael Mastracci, Esquire, Collaborative Divorce Attorney,
Author, *Stop Fighting Over the Kids: Resolving Day-to-Day Custody Conflict in Divorce Situations*

The Intelligent Divorce

Because Your Kids Come First

Book Two:
Taking Care of Yourself

Mark R. Banschick, M.D.

David Tabatsky

Intelligent Book Press

The Intelligent Divorce is not intended as a substitute for psychotherapy or professional consultations in matters of family crisis. Whenever appropriate, we encourage you to seek expert medical help and/or legal advice. *The Intelligent Divorce* should be used only as a general guide and not as the ultimate source of information on divorce.

The author and publisher shall have neither liability nor responsibility to any person or entity with respect to any loss or damage caused, or alleged to have been caused, directly or indirectly, by the information contained in this book.

Throughout the book, you'll discover anecdotal scenarios (EXAMPLE), analytical evaluations ("From the Couch"), and first-person accounts. Without exception, names have been changed or left anonymous.

Published in the United States by Intelligent Book Press
P.O. Box 3098, Stamford, Connecticut 06905

ISBN: 978-0-9825903-2-4

Library of Congress Control Number: 2011906754

Illustrations by Edna Cabcabin Moran
Interior Design by 1106 Design
Cover Design by Cathi Stevenson
Cover Illustration by Jana Guothova, *www.istock.com/lordalea*

In Honor of My Mother,
Helen Banschick

In Memory of My Father,
Sheren Banschick

Contents

Contents

Foreword

The Intelligent Divorce is designed to help parents negotiate the complicated and sometimes unbearable terrain of divorce with dignity, wisdom, and a healthy dose of reality. When parents commit to an intelligent divorce they commit to protecting the innocence of their children. This is the most important reason for writing this book, and we hope it will be your biggest motivation for reading it.

Think of it as an insurance policy for your kids' well-being. People insure homes, cars, and even their own lives against the unpredictability of life's tragic events, reassuring themselves in case something goes wrong. You may be losing your marriage, but you don't have to lose a positive sense of yourself or a healthy relationship with your kids. There are ways to intelligently protect all of you.

As a child psychiatrist and expert witness in custody matters, I have seen how divorce affects each and every member of the family, including siblings, grandparents, and in-laws. But I am convinced that divorce, while admittedly painful, can be done well. A positive outcome is worth the effort—for you, your kids, and yes, even for your ex.

The Intelligent Divorce—Book One: Taking Care of Your Children was devoted to helping parents see divorce through the lens of relationships, both with their (ex) spouses and especially with their children.

Book Two: Taking Care of Yourself revolves around you—the greatest asset your kids have. Despite the inevitable power struggles you may have with your ex, if you do the hard work of staying healthy, centered, and focused on your children's well-being, you'll be pleasantly surprised by how well they'll do. After all, they want to see their mom and dad happy, positive, and communicating effectively with each other. And if you're raising your children alone, this book, along with *Book One*, will help you become a positive role model for your kids.

We're going to help you and your family get through this, one step at a time. We won't ask you to be positive when you're feeling badly. And we can't make you feel good when you simply don't. What we *can* do is equip you with the necessary tools to better understand your situation, handle it to the very best of your ability, and come through it not only intact but healthier, as an individual and as a parent.

This book is divided into three parts.

In *Part One: Conflict, Insights, and Solutions* we will review the basic concepts all parents needs to know in order to protect their kids during a divorce, like dealing with power struggles between parents, establishing and maintaining Intergenerational Boundaries, the dangers of the internet, and some basic rules about parental dating.

In *Part Two: Mind, Body, and Spirit* we will explore the triangle of mind, body, and spirit, beginning with developing a healthy personal psychology to strengthening your body and exploring how you may connect with your spiritual side. This begins with a positive look at grieving and why it's natural and actually good for you. We'll investigate how people often regress in stressful situations, and discuss ten emotional traps that you can avoid. And if your ex-husband or wife is behaving destructively, we will help you with the unenviable task of dealing with their bad choices.

You will also learn about your triggers, those words and actions that drive you nuts, and how to handle them. We'll dive headfirst into anger and anxiety, two powerful emotions that at one time or another cause most of us to misbehave. Research suggests that this becomes easier when you improve your diet and fitness, as well as embracing your personal faith and the power of community.

In *Part Three: Secure, Strong, and Hopeful* we return to raising your children, including how to recognize and deal with childhood regression. This will help you understand your kids and deal with their issues before they become significant problems.

We'll also provide a financial primer and additional insight about your finances as a single parent. And, since men and women handle stress differently, we are including a gender-specific program for dealing with your divorce, including self-assessment tests to honestly gauge your progress. Both of these can help you get through your divorce intact and stronger than ever.

Finally, considering all that you have learned, it's time to declare your own independence, and celebrate it, too.

Whether or not you believe in a divine power that watches over you, this moment in your life counts. How you handle your divorce will be your legacy. It is our prayer for you that one day you will look back at this time (and your kids) with pride for a job well done.

In the twenty-first century, divorce is a choice. And more often than one might imagine, those who are pulled grudgingly into a divorce often find themselves in a better place once they reach the other side. Divorce, like many major life changes, has a beginning, middle, and end, and you *will* find your way.

We hope that this book will become an interactive workbook for you and a support group that you can carry throughout your journey. In fact, we encourage you and your ex to pay close attention to the Parenting Agreement in the back of this book, which both parties can sign and commit their best effort to keeping.

Remember, you are not alone. Help is right here in your hands.

In a spirit of fairness and authenticity we are randomly interchanging the use of male and female examples throughout the book. We are, in effect (and pardon the pun), divorcing ourselves from any perceived gender bias.

The terms "ex" and "ex-spouse" are meant to include those who are preparing for a divorce, in the midst of one, or have already signed off on the entire process.

Part One

Conflict, Insight, and Solutions

We Know You're In There

After a long day at work, I cherish the comforts of home and the beauty of being with my family. As the night comes to an end—after household chores, homework, and whatever else might have become that day's agenda—I love watching my kids get into their pajamas, ready themselves for bed, and pick a book for us to read together. It sounds idyllic, right? For any parent who adores his children, is there anything better than that? In all honesty, I must admit there is.

I sometimes prefer the moment *after* my children are asleep, when I finally have the chance to take care of myself. That window of opportunity is crucial, even in the best of times. It affords me the chance to catch up on my To Do list, ready myself for the day ahead, and if I'm lucky I'll even get to slow down and pay attention to what's most important: my peace of mind.

But for a parent in the midst of a divorce, this time can be unsettling. When a normally challenging day finally ends and life slows down for a moment, that's when you will be reminded of how stressful your life may have become. In fact, if you're not careful, it's incredibly easy to simply lose yourself in the process.

The following image depicts something you see frequently in divorce: individuals whose personal selves are crowded out by what surrounds them. We are quite certain you know what this feels like. It's as if you're always responding to the needs of others, taking care of someone else, and tackling one crisis after another. Meanwhile, is anyone taking care of you?

This second book in our series is dedicated to taking care of you. The image below suggests what can happen when your life is balanced and well put together. The individual in the middle has a clear identity and is equipped to deal effectively with the challenges of a divorce.

By taking charge of your life, you're more likely to be healthy and happy, and your kids will follow suit. We admit that this isn't easy. But once you get started, you create a cycle of positive feedback, one that continues to yield returns.

The better care you take of yourself, the more likely you will be to feel the results and continue in that direction. The better your children feel with you, the easier it will be to parent them in the future. Goodwill counts for a lot, not just with your kids, but with your ex-husband or ex-wife, as well. Trust leads to better co-parenting. And setting good limits, when required, lets a difficult ex know that he has to think twice before misbehaving.

You can't improvise your way through a divorce. You need a plan. That's what we're here for, to help you formulate what will work for you and ultimately for your children. One parent can make a difference, and your good decisions will influence everyone.

Let's begin by examining how power struggles impact nearly every facet of divorce and how guarding the Intergenerational Boundary can protect the innocence of your children. If you come away with nothing else, these two basic principles are worth the price of admission.

CHAPTER 1

Strategies for Parenting under Stress

What Is a Power Struggle?

A power struggle occurs when two people have different opinions and each feels the need to win, often at all costs. Sometimes, it's simply each parent wanting to be heard, respected, and trusted that creates conflict. More often, power struggles emerge when one parent tries to maintain control of a situation out of anxiety or the belief that he or she is right.

Sound familiar? It's no secret that power struggles are a major barrier to a positive divorce experience. You may be fighting about the kids, money, the house, or who is the better parent. The list can seem endless. But when you engage in power struggles merely for the sake of winning, no one really does, especially your children. It's simple: they lose. Understanding this is essential, especially if you agree that you must put your children first.

Divorce can be scary. James Hollis, a noted psychologist, tells us that the opposite of love is fear, not hate, and that when love is taken away, people feel abandoned and scared. Fear engenders powerful reactions that can trigger power struggles.

It takes only one person to start a power struggle, because if one of you engages the other negatively, the other must respond in self-defense. It's a vicious cycle, with mistrust leading to more mistrust, which can spill over into your kids' lives, often with lasting consequences.

Before you get your kids into their pajamas and eventually take time to care for yourself, let's look at some workable methods for dealing with power struggles in a positive way.

Judith's Story

As we were going through our divorce, I realized how important it was to the kids that I be able and willing to develop a civil relationship with their dad. Once they saw Will and me talking peacefully together in the same room, they seemed better. It motivated me. When kids see that every little thing doesn't precipitate war, and that their parents can be polite and civil, it goes a long, long way.

Judith, age 44

Handling Power Struggles with Your Ex-Spouse

When you divorce, your marital partnership is severed, but the innate alliance joining parent and child remains for each of you. This is sacred ground and must somehow be shared. Your kids need both their mom and their dad, and you've got the tough task of working together with someone you may not like and who may also be undermining you at times. When power struggles take over, the natural order is distorted. Kids may become unwilling messengers or witness frightening scenes of anger. They may find themselves forced to take sides or simply be spoiled by an overindulgent (and guilty) parent.

Regardless, you must keep your kids separate from all of this. Their task as children is to follow the normal path of development into healthy adulthood. It's your task, and the task of their other parent, to restructure your family and support normal child development. The easiest way to build that new family is from the ground up, so that's where we'll start, where it's messy and tough, and hard to see the light.

Wounded Souls and Control Freaks Beware

How do you speak nicely to your children about their mother if, because of her, you believe you will never recover financially? Can you co-parent effectively when your children's father continues to see the woman who you feel has destroyed your life? Are you able to hold your tongue in front of your kids when your ex continues to abuse your agreed-upon custody schedule and lies to your kids in order to manipulate them into spending more time away from you?

Does any of this sound familiar? If so, you may be wondering how you can improve your situation. Perspective is the first step, and it's something you've started to gain by reading this book.

You may feel lost, hurt, or unbearably angry, but perspective teaches us that life goes on and these emotions will pass. It also reminds us that protecting yourself is integral to preserving your children's health and happiness. This awareness leads to knowing your boundaries: what you can handle and what you can't; what you're willing to compromise and what you won't allow; and, of course, what treatment you, yourself, are willing to accept. Perspective helps you analyze the situation at hand so that you can recognize when your dignity is at stake and when you're simply overreacting.

EXAMPLE
It's Good That We Can Talk

Vivian is driving her kids to school when she gets word that her close friend's mother has suddenly passed away. The funeral is today, but it's her turn to pick up the kids after school. In a panic, she calls their father.

"Ralph. Something's come up. I need you to get the kids today."

Ralph's thinking, "Here she goes again! Always thinking about herself."

"Sorry Vivian," he says. "I have another obligation."

"Listen Ralph, you have to do this for me. I won't be able to make it today and they need a ride to practice."

"Fine." *Ralph slams the phone so Vivian can hear his frustration.*

Later that evening, Vivian gets the kids from Ralph's place.

"Thanks so much for getting them today, Ralph."

"You know Vivian, you can't just call up and demand that I get the kids whenever it suits you. It's selfish, Viv. That's what it is."

"So you think I'm selfish? Nice. You have no clue."

"Try me."

"I just heard that Sandy's mom passed away while I was in the car with the boys. The funeral was this afternoon so I called you. I didn't want to upset the kids, which is why I didn't say anything."

"Oh! I'm sorry to hear that, Viv. And sorry I misunderstood you. Had I only known I wouldn't have been so upset."

"Yeah."

"Listen, we're in this together. I really am sorry."
"I know. Thanks, Ralph. I'm glad we cleared things up. It's good that we can talk."

"From the Couch"

Ralph and Vivian's divorce isn't perfect. Ralph has lost some faith in Vivian, and his temper flares easily. Nonetheless, they are still talking and working together to put their kids first. Ralph may have been angry that Vivian called him at the last minute, but he still agreed to pick up the boys. He gave her the benefit of the doubt. This turned out to be a good idea.

I hope you noticed that Ralph, when apologizing, pointed out that both he and Vivian were *in this together.* This is a useful technique called *Joining,* which I will review as we get deeper into power struggles and how to minimize them. What we see here is a couple doing their best to work together for the sake of their kids.

During the initial phase of many divorces, trust breaks down, parents lose the faith they had in their former partner, and they often feel guilt and anger. Under these circumstances, no one wants to compromise because the underlying resentments are just too profound. On top of that, neither party is thinking clearly. Fueled by parental disagreement and lack of conciliation, a cycle of negative behavior ensues, which usually leads to more mistrust, eventually spilling over into the lives of the children and injuring their innocence.

EXAMPLE
Did You Say Perspective?

*Vanessa has left Paul after 15 years of mar-
riage. She has also met another man. This comes as*

a complete surprise to Paul, who mistakenly thought his marriage was pretty good. The double whammy of being sued for divorce and losing his wife to another man has left Paul feeling like his life is falling apart. He is bitter about Vanessa's betrayal.

Communication with Vanessa has become increasingly confrontational. Paul almost never misses an opportunity to attack her by cursing, being short, and yelling over nothing, sometimes in front of their kids and even in public.

Although Paul is consulting a lawyer and seeing a therapist, for now he is refusing to begin any settlement proceedings. He wants to force Vanessa to meet with him, face to face, alone, to tell him the truth about why she left the marriage. She has refused, agreeing to meet Paul only in the presence of her lawyers.

"From the Couch"

Unless Paul can get a handle on his controlling anger, nothing much will happen. He and Vanessa are deep into a confrontational power struggle, and boundaries are not being respected. Paul has been hurt, that's for sure, but by playing the role of the victim he is injuring his children. Vanessa, unwilling or unable to deal effectively with her husband, is hiding behind her lawyers. They will probably remain stuck in a cycle of confrontation until Paul gets on with his grieving. Who doesn't feel badly for Paul? But it doesn't change the fact that his kids must come first. And that means Paul can't, under any circumstances, be yelling at their mother in front of them.

EXAMPLE
Stop Bullying Me!

Sabina and Johannes have been married for ten years and have three children. The stress of parenting and two demanding jobs has taken its toll. Unfortunately, they have separated. Initially, they both thought it would be an amicable process, but once litigation began, it was as if they each discovered alternate personalities and couldn't control themselves.

Sabina tried to get the upper hand, claiming she was the only one looking out for the children. Every time she spoke to Johannes she acted as if she was in charge and he was an idiot. When Johannes reacted, she would cut him off and belittle him.

Sabina decided to gain more control by consistently bringing the kids an hour or two late to Johannes for his weekend visits. When he mentioned it, Sabina scoffed at him and suggested he add it to the list he was making with his lawyer to screw her.

Sabina began to make it more and more difficult for Johannes to speak with the children on the phone. She claimed that he was threatening her and that she didn't feel safe. She changed the locks on the house and insisted that Johannes meet the kids at a nearby gas station. Finally, she called the police to falsely report that Johannes was stalking the house.

"From the Couch"

When your ex threatens you, whether it's legally, physically, or psychologically, that's bullying. For some people, it's the only way they know how to establish power and hold on to it. Sabina is an unfortunate example, and Johannes is the unwilling victim. The divorce has brought out the worst in Sabina, but the ones who are really losing out are her children.

As you can see, it's not always the man who is the bully. No one should ever demean or belittle you in order to get her way. You cannot allow it. You must set limits. It may be as simple as telling him or her that you will not continue a nasty conversation. It may mean walking away, or hanging up the phone, or not responding to a provocative email. And in tough cases, setting limits may mean calling the police or an appropriate agency.

If you have been bullied or manipulated over an extended period of time, it may be difficult to recognize this behavior for what it is because it's the way things have always been. This is particularly true if you came from a family in which a father, mother, or sibling was abusive to you. Being bullied can be so much a part of what you expect that you may lack objectivity.

No one benefits from being bullied. The bully ends up with too much power, and the bullied person ends up demeaned. It is something your children don't need to see, for any reason.

A Test

1. How do you and your ex-spouse cope with power struggles?
2. Are you being bullied or manipulated?
3. Are you bullying the mother or father of your children?
4. Do you respect your ex-spouse?
5. Can you and your ex-spouse really put your children first?

The Prognosis

Many individuals don't even recognize their own behavior when they're caught up in a web of power struggles. It's so important that you take a good look at yourself and try to determine your own responsibility for whatever conflict you are having with your ex. Once you do that, you can at least alter your own behavior.

If you feel like you're being bullied or manipulated, it will help if you can determine why your ex is behaving that way. Perhaps you are provoking each other and a shift in your attitude may relax the situation. Or maybe your ex is out of control and you will need to seek professional help. In either case, an honest assessment of the situation will do you the most good.

Your divorce can become a positive experience only when parents share some level of mutual respect. But if you don't have a willing partner, you simply can't pull it off, no matter how hard you try. If that's your situation your goal is to reduce the intensity of these power struggles rather than try to eliminate them entirely. Better to be realistic than naively hopeful.

Either way, it's not easy. You have to first establish your role in the conflicts you are having. Are you "triggering" your ex? If so, you'll need to learn how to modify your behavior. And if your ex is determined to win, no matter what, you will need to find the strength to avoid getting sucked in to his or her games.

Remember: You can only control your own feelings and behavior. So if your spouse is not respecting you, don't let that become an excuse for losing self-respect. Your own dignity and confidence will go a long way toward helping you and your children cope with divorce. Finally, if and when respect is sorely lacking, the most dignified thing you can do is set clear limits and avoid further mistreatment.

Effective techniques exist for improving communication skills with your ex-spouse. On the following pages, you will discover specific tips for coping with the communication struggles divorce can present. Feel free to copy this material and hold on to it for future reference. You never know when you may need to stop for a moment so you can decide how to respond effectively to something your ex has said or done.

Getting Beyond Perpetual Conflict

First and foremost, you need to understand the needs of your children. No matter what the issue might be, the way you approach your ex-spouse must be done with your children's well-being and best interests in mind. At the same time, it's important to remember that your ex cares about the kids, too. Before approaching him, even about what may seem like a simple matter, ask yourself if your intended approach is a healthy one, and if not, is there an alternative way to communicate without triggering a negative reaction? By considering these factors before initiating communication, you can put yourself in a more assertive position and even the playing field. In this way, when it is used judiciously, power can be healthy.

Perspective

Preparing yourself for conflict pays off most of the time. You can reclaim real power in the endless power struggles of divorce by maintaining your focus on the welfare of your children. This is hard to do by yourself because few people maintain objectivity when it comes to the reasoning behind their actions.

Perspective will help you know when to listen carefully and compromise and when to set limits or get outside help, if needed. Perspective will help you feel centered about what you are doing and guide you toward making good decisions that are best for your kids. After all, it's not just about winning another round in an endless power struggle. Once you realize this and operate accordingly, you may actually have real power to do some good.

Active Listening and Effective Communication

Active listening is a set of techniques designed to slow down hostility and anxiety in the present moment. It introduces something that's often lost when a marriage falls apart—the willingness to respectfully listen to one another. Active listening defuses reactivity and ongoing power struggles. It includes joining, curiosity, mirroring, clarification, and two additional techniques called sticking to the problem at hand and striking when the iron is cold.

Joining

Joining occurs when you remind your ex that the two of you are "in this together" for the sake of the kids. In the heat of an argument, this statement can defuse tension and get you back on track.

"Michael relax, I want to remind you that we're in this together."
"Rachel, I know you worry about the children. I do, too."

Curiosity

Curiosity can play an important role in building positive communication by turning polarizing power struggles into healthier collaborations. Curiosity can open the door to something good.

"Let's start fresh. What's the best way to handle this problem?"

"Let me tell you what is going on in my house. What do you think?"

You might also consider expressing curiosity over your own behaviors. Establish between the two of you what bothers your ex, and perhaps you may even ask for suggestions on how to change. Who knows? She may reciprocate and try to adjust to your needs, as well.

(Some of you may be snickering as you read this advice, and if so, you should really be asking yourself how willing you are to communicate honestly and contemplate change, yourself.)

Mirroring

Mirroring diffuses the callousness and absurdity of over-heated accusations. If one party is acting harshly, you can choose to mirror back what's been said in less dramatic terms.

"Did you just suggest that I don't care at all about the kids?"

"Let me see if I understand what you just said; I always do the wrong thing?"

Don't be smug or cynical when mirroring, otherwise you'll lose the value of the intervention. Mirroring gives you both an opportunity to take a step back and regroup in the midst of a conversation. Sometimes it can get you back on track and limit the damage of a power struggle that serves no good purpose.

Clarification

Clarification works by getting you to assume less and listen more. It is predicated on the notion that you don't yet really know what your ex-husband wants to say (even when you think you do). Many unnecessary fights can be averted if you ask specific questions intended to clarify what he really means.

Like mirroring, clarification slows down the power struggle by encouraging a more nuanced conversation.

"What exactly are you trying to tell me? I want you to clarify some details."

"Here are the consequences of this idea; do you see it this way, too?"

Clarifying is different from mirroring. When you mirror, your goal is to get the other individual to hear what he or she has just said. When you engage in clarification, you do so with the desire to understand and cut down your assumptions. Clarification slows down reflexive, negative responses. Even when you don't think you could possibly be at fault, take a step back and suspend any pre-judgment you may usually have.

Sticking to the Problem at Hand

Sticking to the problem at hand means not bringing up old stuff when you're trying to figure out some issue about your children. When you're having an argument with your ex-spouse, it's a good idea to stay focused on what you want to solve, right then and there.

You have endless stories from the past stored in your head—he did this, she didn't do that, and no matter what, he or she always got it wrong. These old stories rarely help when it comes to working together to raise kids. Someone has to consult with Johnny's teacher so decide what you want to do (together) and keep the bickering to a minimum.

Put your kids first!

Striking When the Iron is Cold

Striking when the iron is cold means trying to deal with difficult problems when you are not upset. Since you already know that certain power struggles tend to induce fights, it's probably best to discuss those toxic issues when you and your ex are not in the middle of dealing with them.

If possible, you should schedule regular time to review how the kids are doing and what needs to be done going forward. We strongly advocate ongoing, non-confrontational meetings in our Parenting Agreement at the end of this book. Engage a third party, like a therapist, if you can't do it on your own.

Setting Limits

This is crucial. If you can't set limits when it's necessary you will never really feel safe with your ex-spouse. Even the best divorce relationships need limits every now and then. For one thing, if you are about to lose control, remove yourself from the situation.

If you are worried about your safety or feel bullied by your former partner, do not allow her behavior to continue and inform her that you have reached your limit. You can do that by telling her that you are going to stop the conversation because it is no longer productive and then proceed to hang up the phone. You can ask a badly behaved ex to leave, or let him know that a particular issue will be better handled between attorneys or with some other third-party present, such as a mediator or therapist.

If you are really threatened, then it is a good idea to have a backup plan that includes your lawyer, other authorities, or even the police. Setting limits keeps a power struggle from deteriorating into something dangerous. If you need to regularly set limits, it is a good idea to have an experienced therapist guide you through your best options. This will help you keep perspective. We will be discussing more about setting limits in subsequent chapters.

Handling Stress

It's not just power struggles with your ex that can stress you out to no end. Divorce challenges your stability, confidence, and self-esteem. All three can lead to an endless cycle of stress, and it behooves you to avoid denial and address each issue.

Do I have the right lawyer? How will I afford to live?
I can't trust him with anything! She's taking everything!
What's going to happen to the kids?
Will I be alone for the rest of my life?

Divorce fills you with thoughts that won't let go, but you still have to parent your kids the best you can. It's a tall order and you are not always going to get it right. But it's doable.

Taking care of yourself is essential. Make a plan. Use common sense. Exercise. Eat well. Stay close to good friends and the people who really care about you. Get therapy. It is good to have an objective person with whom you can process some of your more unpleasant thoughts.

If you are very anxious or inching toward depression, you may want to consider medication for a short period. As a psychiatrist, I frequently prescribe pharmaceuticals with good results. The key is to find a doctor you trust and find medication that works. You can find out more about this in the Resources section in the back of this book, under "Common Psychological and Personality Disorders" and "The Intelligent Consumer: A Guide to Psychiatric Medicine."

Remember: stress is inevitable; falling apart is not.

In case you had forgotten, your children are looking at you for leadership. So take a deep breath and focus on setting a good example. Good habits are contagious. Who knows? You may just convince yourself, too!

Notes

This space is for you—to remember what's important, to doodle, to make plans …

CHAPTER 2

Protecting the Innocence
of Your Children

Insuring Your Kids a Healthy Childhood

You've just learned that with some effort you can manage power struggles with your ex-spouse more adroitly. But the relationship between you and your children requires at least as much attention, if not more. In this chapter, we will explore how to keep your children innocent, healthy, and on track, even when you may be struggling.

Consider the adult and child members of your family. Imagine an invisible line between the adult generation and the children's generation. This line is called the *Intergenerational Boundary*. It's built on one central theme: children must remain children. They're not meant to be exposed to parental conflict or collusion. Children don't need to know too much about the adult world; there's plenty of time for that later, when they grow up. Our kids are best off when they are not our friends. In successful parenting, whether in marriage or divorce, creating and maintaining boundaries will protect and preserve the innocence of our children.

This is easier said than done. Most kids are masters of manipulation, using a variety of strategies, including befriending a parent, splitting the parenting team, and pushing parents to the point of exasperation, where they just give in. All of this can occur in the healthiest of marriages.

In divorce, traditional boundaries are particularly vulnerable. Parents inappropriately confide in their kids. Parents are often needy and the child can be thrown into the role of "parenting" her mother or father. Parents might vie for a child's closeness as part of a desire to hurt the other parent.

Common boundary breaches include fighting when the children are around, talking badly about the other parent in front of the children, and revealing details of your adult life. Even worse are situations when a desperate parent latches on to his kids as a means for support or as a way to hurt the other parent.

You don't want your children to get the message, "I'm your friend," in place of the proper, "I'm your parent." No matter how justified your actions and words may be in the adult world, they have no place on the other side of the Intergenerational Boundary. Children need their parents to act like their parents. They can make new friends anytime.

If all of this sounds simple, it unfortunately isn't. All parents, married or not, struggle to maintain this important boundary, and it's not only because they lack self-control; it's because kids want what they want. Young children may want toys, older children may want to stay up late, and adolescents may want to get away with drinking, smoking weed, or coming home after curfew. Your kids may try to befriend you or your ex or try to drive a wedge between the two of you in order to get their way. You gotta love 'em, but young people are masterminds, and separated moms and dads must be careful to maintain their appropriate parenting role.

Oh My God! I've Become My Mother!

Every family functions like a miniature private society. The art (you mean my parents were artistic?) of raising kids is passed down from parent to child. The quality of this passage, this circle of life, if you will, is up to you.

Your children look to you for cues, and for divorced couples, this can be especially daunting. You don't want your kids exposed to ill will and bad behavior, lest they internalize these techniques and practice them in due time. You also don't want to give up on your restructured family; it can engender a perpetual fear in your children that, when the going gets tough or they do something wrong, people will cut them off.

For better or for worse, everyone learns parenting from his or her own parents. In good marriages, this makes for useful conflict. One parent may deal with a particular issue better than the other, and vice versa. Because many problems can arise that have their origins in the distant past, a divorcing couple should be extra mindful not to repeat old mistakes. Whatever happened in the past to you or your ex-partner need not be repeated with your own children.

EXAMPLE
The Sperm Donor

Gary left his wife, Carolyn, for another woman. Preoccupied by his new "lease on life," he often neglected his three-year-old daughter, Rachel. This left Carolyn feeling irate and bitter, and she had trouble keeping her mouth shut. As a result, Rachel often overheard some rather spicy talk between Mommy and her friends.

"I can't believe what Gary did to you," Carolyn's friend April complained.

"Don't refer to him as Gary," Carolyn replied. "It's much too flattering."

"What do you mean?" April asked.

> *"Rachel's dad is just the sperm donor," Carolyn said.*
>
> *April laughed. "I can't believe what that 'sperm donor' did to you."*
>
> *"Don't worry," Carolyn said. "He'll get his one day."*
>
> *Four years later, Rachel, now seven, is obviously bothered by something. While she and Carolyn are preparing for her weekly visit with her father, Rachel speaks up.*
>
> *"Mommy, why did you call Daddy a sperm donor?"*
>
> *"What?" Carolyn asks, shocked to hear Rachel say such a thing.*
>
> *"Mommy, what is a sperm donor?"*

"From the Couch"

Children like Rachel have uncanny memories (at the most unexpected times) but often struggle to put things in context. With that in mind, it's important to limit any negative moments and build good memories with your children by paying attention to what you do and say. For Carolyn, referring to her deceitful ex-husband as a "sperm donor" was gallows humor, and little more. For Rachel, her mother's comment said something important about her dad, and the memory stuck.

But there was no good reason for Caroline to give her daughter disrespectful images of her father. *Children remember.* Even if you forget what you said, they don't. Caroline needs to remind herself that parenting under stress isn't easy and that protecting her daughter's innocence is her top priority. Loving her child and maintaining a healthy perspective on her divorce will be Caroline's best preventative medicine.

EXAMPLE
Discretion Required

Seth and Linda share joint custody of their ten-year-old son, Ben. Seth is frustrated with Linda's parenting and plans to fight for full custody.

Currently, Ben is with his dad for the weekend. Father and son go to the park to play baseball. While there, Seth bumps into a close friend, Max. Seth takes a break to talk to Max, and Ben, who foresees a boring conversation, asks for a dollar to get ice cream. On the way back, Ben walks up to his dad, who is loudly divulging Linda's incompetent parenting to Max:

"Linda can't even balance a check book. She is completely irresponsible. How can she be trusted as a mother?"

Ben's face flushes, but he continues to listen.

"I don't trust her with Ben. There's no way a judge would either if he knew how reckless and unreliable she really is. She's not cut out to care for my kid."

Ben no longer wants his ice cream.

"From the Couch"

With Ben obviously standing in earshot, Seth is guilty of crossing the Intergenerational Boundary. Ben is ten years old. He should not have been exposed to this adult conversation. He should not have heard his father speak with such disgust about his mother.

How does Ben now know what to believe? His father wants the best for him, but so does his mom—or does she? Ben is only a child; he needn't be forced into the position of doubting his mother's ability to care for him.

Had the Intergenerational Boundary been securely in place, Seth would have shifted the discussion away from Linda the minute he saw Ben approaching. Seth and Max could have continued their talk later, without Ben as their audience.

On which side of the Intergenerational Boundary do you stand? How about your child? Remember: children must remain children. It's their right, and it's your first priority.

Are You Identifying Too Much with Your Children?

It's natural to enjoy our children because they remind us of what it was like when we were young. From their initial baby steps to their first day of school, we can share in their love for the merry-go-round of life. If we're particularly courageous, we can even enjoy it when they ask us for the keys to our car.

Yet there is a downside to this love affair. We can overidentify with our kids and project too much of ourselves onto them. This is not good because our sons and daughters deserve to be who they are. They are not simply extensions of us.

In the case of a divorce, be cautious. Just because you're angry at, or hurt by, their mother or father, doesn't mean your kids should be, too. They deserve the freedom to cultivate their own relationships and discover how they will evolve.

EXAMPLE
Why Does Tony Want to See His Dad?

Holly's husband, Carl, has left her. He was narcissistic, self-involved, and didn't really care about anybody. He worked all the time and put his family at the bottom of his obligation list.

Holly is okay. She is free from a guy who really didn't love her, and when Tony, their nine-year-old son, keeps asking to see his dad, Holly just doesn't get it.

"He was such a jerk to us," she tells him.

Tony replies, "Mommy stop it, I don't care!" He walks away.

"What do you mean?" Holly asks. "How could you not care?"

One day, Carl calls with tickets to see a great game. Holly yells into the phone, "Tony doesn't want to go out with you! Where were you last week? Who cares about these tickets?!"

Tony cries, "Mommy, I want to be with my dad!"

"From the Couch"

Holly is right. Carl is a narcissistic, self-absorbed father, and he probably hasn't given his all to his son. Holly tries to protect Tony by pushing Carl away but, as much as she thinks she is doing the right thing, she is making a mistake. Holly is overidentifying with Tony; Carl may have neglected her, but that doesn't mean he will neglect their son the same way. She has to let go and allow Tony to develop his own relationship with his father. (By the way, Tony and Carl had a good time at the game.)

Displacement: When You Wanna Kick the Dog

Have you ever noticed that when you're upset about something (your boss wasn't nice to you or someone stood you up) you make the mistake of redirecting your stress elsewhere? You come home, you're irritable, and your kids don't have to do a lot wrong for you to let them have it.

This is called *displacement*. It's when your irritation moves from one source to another, in this case, to your children. Some people let their frustration out by hitting a punching bag or by banging the pots and pans in the kitchen. These methods of release are pretty benign. But displacement can be truly destructive, and in divorce, it can be devastating. The stress and your subsequent bad behavior can cause a lot of damage. You're angry and you're irritable, and you just can't take it anymore. We know that, at times, you're going to let loose on your kids. It's not right, but it is what it is.

I encourage you to have perspective and to set limits with yourself. If you walk into the house pissed off at your ex-wife, mad at your boss, at your mother-in-law, or at the IRS, wait a bit, so you don't say anything harsh to your son or daughter. The Intergenerational Boundary requires that you protect him or her from inappropriate anger.

EXAMPLE
Mom's Mad

Mom: "Stephen—will you come up here?"
Stephen: "Hold on a minute, Mom."
Mom: "Stephen!"

Stephen is quiet. He is on Facebook.
Mom: "Stephen!!!!"
No response.
Mom: "You better come up here! I've had a long day."
Stephen: "Mom! Stop yelling, I'm on my way!"
Mom: "Stop yelling? Don't start with me young man!"
Stephen: "Mom! Stop!"
Mom: "You're lazy, just like your father."
Stephen: "Mom!"
Mom: "Were you on Facebook? Why are you crying, Stephen?"

"From the Couch"

Stephen is a preoccupied teenage boy. He might seem annoying, but he is normal. He needs to be corrected but he doesn't need to experience his mother's rage or be compared to his father in a negative light. Mom's rant can backfire in a number of ways. It can make Stephen dislike his father. It can make him angry at her. Neither one is useful.

When you're upset about something else, protect the Intergenerational Boundary and leave your kids alone. If they deserve correction, give it to them when you're back on your game.

What's Love Got to Do with It?

You don't have to love or even like your ex in order to protect the Intergenerational Boundary. It helps to get along, but it's even better when you're disciplined in your approach to parenting. Children are more likely to do well when they see that their mom and dad have a good relationship, but the real requirement for their healthy growth is that you keep the conflict out of their lives.

EXAMPLE
Violet and Mason Get Their Priorities Straight

Violet and Mason are going through an ugly separation, which isn't surprising because their marriage had been miserable from the start.

Mason was no angel. He had more than one affair, including a tryst with a prostitute. Violet was loyal, but never loyal to his feelings; she never really seemed to care about him.

Their two children, Ian (16) and Mia (11), are faring well. Despite the animosity, Violet and Mason are disciplined in their commitment to their children. They appear in court regularly and each can barely stand the other's presence, but when it comes to the kids, they have stepped up.

Violet finds herself wanting to tell Mia about her father's "disgusting" behavior. But she doesn't. Mason wants to roll his eyes whenever Ian complains about his mother's irritating ways, but he refrains.

"From the Couch"

Despite fierce animosity and, at times, downright hatred, Violet and Mason are doing something sacred: they are prioritizing the innocence of their children.

It would be so easy for Violet to turn her kids against their dad, but she doesn't. It would be even easier for Mason to roll his eyes along with his son, but he'll have no part of it.

Protecting the Intergenerational Boundary is not about being nice and sweet. It's about action. Kids are not to hear about your feelings of contempt, or lack of respect, for their mom or dad. In this way, Violet and Mason are performing like Olympic athletes against all odds. You don't have to like your ex in order to provide your children with what they need. Violet and Mason are to be applauded.

EXAMPLE
Picture Perfect?

Jackson and Amber have four kids: Cameron (17), Jacob (15), Grace (10), and Olivia (7). Like most people, they have had their problems going through their divorce. It took a long time to agree on a monetary settlement and on custody arrangements, but through it all, they prioritized their kids' needs.

Amber recently discovered that Jackson has been dating one of her (so-called) friends. She isn't happy about it; in fact, she's downright upset, but since she's the one who wanted the divorce in the first place she figures she has to accept it as one of the consequences. She also knows she can't let her feelings get in the way of a bigger problem that's surfaced: Cameron is using drugs.

Jackson discovered it first. He noticed that Cameron's clothes smelled and that he was acting out of character. Amber had been so busy working out a plan to help Olivia in school (she has learning disabilities) that she hadn't noticed.

In spite of their difficulties, Amber and Jackson pulled together. They circled the wagons, hired a therapist, and have started talking frequently about Cameron's progress. Their children have noticed their cooperative behavior and are responding well. Despite his best efforts, Cameron cannot split his parents apart.

"From the Couch"

Amber and Jackson made a commitment not to badmouth each other in front of the kids. If they had issues, they agreed to deal with them privately.

Knowing that Jackson was dating someone who had been close to her wasn't easy for Amber, but she knew that at the end of the day it was more important that she and Jackson sustain their feelings of good will. This kind of mindset is important because Mom and Dad have to be on the same team. In this case, it's crucial: Cameron and Olivia need all the help and support they can get. Instead of blaming the other parent, this couple worked together. The result? Four healthy children and better sleep at night for each parent.

Preventing Unnecessary Mistakes

Your kids look up to you. If you handle yourself with dignity and strength, your kids will naturally follow your lead. Living a positive, happy life, despite the stress, is a great message—if you have difficulty finding your way there, get the help you need to step up to the task.

The Intergenerational Boundary is present in everything you do. It's evident in the way you speak to other parents on the playground, in how you shop for food while your little child is in the cart, or in the risqué laundry you absentmindedly leave out in plain sight for all to see. Any time your kids have even the slightest chance of observing your behavior, you must consider the Intergenerational Boundary and make every effort to be a good role model.

This brings us to three important topics: dating, the internet, and what to tell your kids.

Keeping New Relationships Private

You want to surround your kids with caring adults, but introducing a new love interest into the lives of your children before they are ready will most likely be detrimental.

You may have left your marriage and literally walked into the arms of another woman or a new boyfriend. Perhaps your new friend gave you the courage to leave. We're not going to sit in judgment. What's important is that you recognize your child's need to remain innocent and that you make every effort to help your ex-spouse maintain his or her dignity.

Whether you're seeing someone right now, or will be seeing someone in the future, your kids need not know about it right away. It is confusing for them when they have to deal with your new love interest. It upsets their grieving process and can break them out of healthy denial.

If they feel forced to choose, they may decide to hate you and support their other parent, who can use the situation to further manipulate the kids to their side. It's also possible that they'll hate your new love interest, and if you choose to marry, it may be a disaster. Your kids may never come around.

If your children ask you about dating, you can tell them that it's not something you're discussing right now. You can let them know that if you have someone new to introduce to them, you will do so when you're ready and only when it's serious.

People ask me when it's time. My answer is: not for a long while. Wait until things have settled down. Take at least six months, or even better, a year or more. Wait until you're living in separate places and the kids have found their center. Most important, wait until you're sure that this relationship is going to be stable. You don't want numerous Janes and Joes marching through your children's lives. It may make you feel good, but it's unsettling for them.

It *is* easy to slip, and we get it. You enjoy someone else's company, and you want him around. After all, you were unhappy in your marriage, so why can't you be happy now?

It takes discipline to remain on your side of the Intergenerational Boundary. Be patient. Enjoy your relationship on your time—not your kid's—and determine whether it's serious. You'll have nights and weekends to see if this is going to work.

Protecting Your Family Computer

Managing your communication devices is essential if you want a shot at keeping things private. You may not have control over your ex or his desire to remain in your kids' lives, but you do have full reign over your own behavior. Because it can have such damaging effects on your children, it's important that we discuss access to adult content and its unintended consequences.

Too many parents think that their kids won't see what they're doing on the computer, but make no mistake, children are technology masters and their curiosity is boundless. I've seen many, many cases of kids who have been injured because of their parents' irresponsible behavior at the computer. Don't be naïve. Kids can easily break into their parent's email or search through the history of their parent's internet activity. It rarely turns out well.

EXAMPLE
A Child's Curiosity

Hal and Sherry divorced two years ago. Most of the time, the kids (Ella, age 11, Ashley, age 9, and Landon, age 6) lived with their mom, so at night, when Hal was lonely, he scanned the internet for pornography.

Hal has downloaded a number of videos and images, and they sit in unlocked folders on his computer desktop.

Ashley, like most kids, is intensely curious. She gets into everything. So it came as no surprise when she broke through Hal's passwords (it wasn't hard—he wasn't savvy and used his birthday) and accessed his desktop. She was shocked to find pictures of naked women having sex with men, among other activities. She shut down the computer quickly and didn't tell a soul.

"From the Couch"

How does Ashley get over this?

As adults, we can choose whether to judge Hal, and most of us probably won't. Viewing pornography is legal in your own home. Hal certainly didn't intend for his children to see it.

But look at the unintended consequences for his daughter. What are her memories of this moment as she moves forward and develops sexually? How does she process what she has seen? This huge burden was created in one moment, and it all could have been avoided.

Protecting your children's innocence requires vigilance and savvy. Be careful about online communications. You don't want your children burdened with, or shocked by, your private life. Whether you're watching internet porn, chatting with a girlfriend about your anger toward your children's father, or having a secret relationship, don't be surprised if your kids tap into any of your computer activities. All of this demands your strict attention and utmost discretion.

Telling Your Kids

Before we move on to focus on how you can take better care of yourself, there is one more piece of unfinished business. This entire book is based upon putting your kids first. So, what about the big elephant in the room—telling your kids about the divorce?

It's probably the hardest thing you will ever have to do.

Think carefully about picking the right time and make a real effort to collaborate with your ex. This will be an important moment in the life of your family and you basically have one chance to get it right.

Here are a list of Do's and Don'ts to make the big day a bit easier.

Please Note:
If you want to know more about the "big day," we provide an in depth discussion in *The Intelligent Divorce— Book One: Taking Care of Your Children.*

Do's

1. Make it totally clear that the divorce is not their fault.
2. Keep your confidants (friends and family) to a minimum during this process.
3. Do this together with your spouse (if possible).
4. Plan ahead for what you want to say.
5. Provide as much practical information as possible.
6. Control your feelings and stay on top of things.
7. Let your children ask questions.
8. Remind them that life will eventually get better.
9. Be hopeful and positive.
10. Be the adult. Let your kids be kids.

Don'ts

1. Don't drag your feet in telling your children.
2. Don't let anyone else announce the news.
3. Don't play the blame game (there's probably plenty to go around).
4. Don't air your dirty laundry in front of your kids.
5. Don't let your emotions get the best of you.
6. Don't reveal more than is appropriate.
7. Don't lie. It will always catch up to you later.
8. Don't put your kids in the position of having to take sides.
9. Don't forget to remind them that your divorce is not their fault.
10. Don't improvise. You have one chance to get it right.

Notes

This space is for you—to remember what's important, to doodle, to make plans …

Part Two
Mind, Body, and Spirit

Before and After

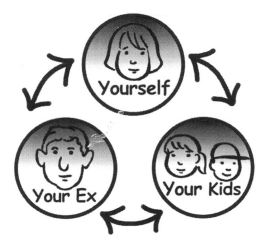

The triangle shown here could be viewed as a three-legged stool, with each one dependent on the other. Let's consider that a metaphor for a healthy family, whether intact under a single roof or living positively with the outcome of a divorce.

You, your ex, and your kids are in a dynamic relationship with one another, and will be for years to come. And *you* are the one person in this group over which you have the most control. When you know yourself, you know how much you can handle—when to say yes and when to say no. When you're centered, you can deal with almost any ex, even the most difficult one, and you'll be better able to parent your kids. They need to know that you can take care of yourself—so that they don't have to!

After all, what good is a mother to her children if she is always tired and irritable? What about a dad who is so obsessed with his divorce that he can't stay focused while driving, putting his family at risk? When you lose sight of yourself, you shut down.

We're not encouraging narcissism; we're encouraging you to find your center. Without it, everything becomes more difficult. You have more power than you think, even if your divorce seems out of control. I am certain that your insight, your good energy, and your actions have the ability to affect the nature of this process and to protect your kids' precious childhood.

In the next few chapters, you'll figure out many of the emotions that may be assaulting your senses. Once you get a handle on them, you can begin to heal your mind, body, and spirit. Remember, taking time for yourself isn't selfish. It's what's necessary to ensure that you are at your best during this crucial time.

CHAPTER 3

When Normal Parents Fall Apart: The Psychology of Loss and Regression

Divorce can be dangerous.

Breaking Up Is Hard to Do

Healthy people are going to be upset about divorce. It's painful when you lose something that was so important to you. Even if you're excited about new opportunities, it is human to grieve, both for yourself and for what your children could have had if things had worked out differently.

In this chapter, we focus on what you're going through. We'll walk you carefully through grief: why you're feeling it, what makes it good for you, and how to get through it. Then we'll take a close look at what happens when your mind and emotions slip—it's a phenomenon called regression. Not everyone regresses in divorce, just 99 percent of everyone. By understanding how you regress and how it can cost you and your children, you can gain control. First, let's look at what you're going through.

Understanding Grief: Because It's Good for You to Be Feeling Something

Grief is positive; it's part of healing. If you bang your toe and it bruises or bleeds, your physiological reaction is part of the recovery process. The pain you feel is a signal to be tender with your toe—not to test it. Swelling tells you that your immune system is taking charge, and bruising reminds you that it will take time to heal. You know that if you bandage your wound properly, keep it clean, and allow nature to do its thing, you will heal, and you'll heal well.

So, too, with emotional wounds. Grief is our psychological immune system at work; it allows our spirit to nurse itself back to life. Now, if you're the "leaver," you may feel relief and elation. Your grief may be minor. We will counsel you to be pragmatic for the sake of your children; they are going to need your attention and care. If, however, you're the "leave-ee," the one who has been left, you're probably holding a bag of resentment, hurt, and maybe even fear. You're swollen with emotion and, in response, you may want to sleep and avoid, or simply attack. In my experience, there are really no words to express just how wounded you may feel.

This is all part of the grieving process and, ultimately, it's all for the best. Grief is the natural, psychological response to the loss of a marriage, and you need to go through it in order to come out of your divorce healthy and strong.

Grief slows you down so you can appreciate what you had, digest your hurt, and, ultimately, focus on the future. Toward that end, it may even affect you physiologically. You may lose your appetite or become ravenous, or have difficulty falling or staying asleep. This is your mind telling you that it needs time to heal, and by managing your divorce intelligently—perhaps with guidance from a minister, pastor, rabbi, or therapist—you *will* heal. It bears repeating: grief is a positive thing.

The following two lists will help you visualize your mind's immune reaction. For each stage on the left, enumerating the stages of the body's healing process, there is a corresponding stage on the right, describing the mind's therapeutic equivalent for psychological wounds.

Physical Wound	Psychological Wound
Bleeding	Loss/Betrayal/Hurt
Physical Pain	Psychological Pain
Tenderness	Tender Feelings/ Need to Self-Protect
Dressing	Kind Friends/Loving Family/ Self-Care
Bandage	Protecting Yourself/Setting Good Limits/ Legal Counsel (when necessary)
Healing Over Time	Healing Over Time

To give you a more concrete guide to your psychological immune system, we're going to review a model for grief that was described by Elisabeth Kübler-Ross. She observed the way people grieve when they lose a spouse, child, or parent, and she noted that there was a natural progression inherent in the process.

You may not feel all of the stages of grief, and they won't necessarily happen for you in the given order. You may backtrack, whether for a moment, a day, or a week, and then pop back into a more progressed emotional state soon after. The stages are not a fixed prescription for handling grief. They are an anatomy of the process and a tool for better understanding.

The Five Stages of Grief

Denial

Anger

Bargaining

Depression

Acceptance

Denial

The human mind is designed to combat tough situations, and denial is one of its most common methods. Denial can be adaptive on a short-term basis because in order to function under stress you sometimes have to believe that things are not as serious as they really are.

For example, a study of patients in a Cardiac Care Unit (CCU) found that those in denial (patients believing they were okay) fared better than those who had accepted their fate. Denial played a protective role, giving patients the optimism they needed to assist in their recovery.

While you know and understand that you are going through divorce, you may, in fact, simultaneously deny that truth. You can tell yourself that the divorce is not really happening or that it will not be that difficult. In divorce, denial can be temporarily useful, but you need to realize that the most functional way to deal with change and hurt is realistically. If you ignore a problem for too long, whether it's a struggling kid or an ex who is acting maliciously, it will only make things worse. After all, those people in the CCU were not taking care of themselves: they had doctors and nurses monitoring their conditions. If something went wrong—if their blood pressure spiked or if they had an arrhythmia—there were professionals to ensure proper treatment. Whether you like it or not, you are in the driver's seat of your divorce. You need to be awake so that you can take care of yourself, make good decisions, and know when it's time to seek outside help.

Anger

When denial no longer works, you'll probably experience anger, directed at either your ex-spouse or at yourself. Sometimes, when you're irritable, you may dump it on your kids.

Anger is almost unavoidable. The disappointment, and sometimes the feeling of betrayal, can be so profound that you find yourself overwhelmed with hostility and sometimes with rage.

"How could he do this to me?"

"I gave her the best years of my life."

"She's gonna pay for this!"

"I will get every single penny out of that bastard!"

55

Anger also opens the door to existential indignation:
"This isn't fair! My friends are happy, why couldn't I be?"
"I don't deserve this. What did I do wrong?"

Beyond your feelings about your ex, you're angry because, though you tried your best, your family vision didn't work out as planned.

But anger is functional, too. It can mobilize you to protect yourself and your children, legally and emotionally. Like a siren making a call to action, anger gets you up, alert, and doing something. It compels you to clarify your boundaries and set stronger limits.

Use your anger constructively; overreacting can make the divorce harder for you and your children—and more expensive too!

Bargaining

Divorce demands such drastic changes that you might at some point feel a strong urge to work it all out with your ex and to have things go back to the way they were. During this stage, you feel the impulse to make nice. You want to concede. You hope beyond hope that it will all be okay—that your relationship was not as bad as you thought.

If you are feeling this way, you might start bargaining with your ex in a manner that is not constructive. Maybe he will relent and come back. Maybe she really still loves you and, with enough coaxing, everything will return to normal. After all, you may tell him or her, you've changed, and your marriage will be okay now. Bargaining sometimes works, but it can backfire if your ex is set on divorce.

You, in fact, might prefer a divorce. It's just that you may not have admitted that yet.

EXAMPLE
Jimmy's Been Had

Kate decided it was time to divorce Jimmy after 12 years of marriage. He was the breadwinner and she was a stay-at-home mom with a part-time job. They had two kids.

After Jimmy caught Kate in an affair, she agreed to go for couples counseling. She didn't miss any appointments, but in her heart of hearts, she was just biding her time to get out.

After six months of counseling, Kate announced that she was prepared to leave the house. She had arranged to live with her new boyfriend.

Jimmy asks, "What about all this counseling?"

Kate answers, "It just didn't work out, Jimmy."

Jimmy feels like he's been had.

"From the Couch"

We can't know Kate's mindset with certainty. Perhaps she was moderately interested in couples counseling. But some people do use counseling as a way to ease out of a marriage. In some cases, this might be a good thing. It gives the leave-ee time to metabolize the loss.

But Jimmy can't be happy about this. He spent six months in therapy and was in denial about Kate's lack of commitment to the marriage. Along with his resentment, he now feels used. In retrospect, it might have been better for Jimmy to come to the realization that Kate wasn't serious about making their marriage work. Sometimes, you just need to cut your losses.

As a psychiatrist, I believe in the value of psychotherapy. But there are cases when a party who really doesn't want to work things out uses it as a manipulative tool. People like this are biding their time and waiting to get out of the marriage at the right moment. Deceit undermines the whole project.

Bargaining, at its core, embraces hope that things can work out, or be better, or sometimes be fixed. That's what Jimmy was looking for. While hope is important, indeed crucial, it needs to be applied realistically. If the marriage can be resuscitated and revitalized, then bargaining pays off. If the marriage is over, then bargaining is a respite between denial and the pain of anger and depression.

Depression

Lord Alfred Tennyson said, "'Tis better to have loved and lost than never to have loved at all."

Is it? When you accept that your life is going to change irrevocably, the heaviness of your loss may hit you hard. This doesn't happen to everyone, but beware the power of depressed feelings; they're natural in grief. When dropping into the depressed stage, a person loses energy, sleeps too much or too little, loses appetite, and fails to find pleasure in the things that he or she used to enjoy. In depression, people find themselves in low moods and can be tearful or want to withdraw from life.

Freud teaches that the element of depression in grief actually has a powerful healing quality to it. It's the process by which the mind lets go of the loss and holds on to positive memories.

When you married someone there was love, once upon a time. Perhaps you and your ex were high school sweethearts, or you recall pulling all-nighters together in college. There's a good chance that you were there for each other through the death of parents or the joyful birth of your children. Divorce isn't simple. You may hate him, but there was probably some good in the marriage—maybe more than just a little bit.

Memories endure. The pleasure of your children remains with you forever. What's required is that you somehow unload the hurt, disappointment, and emptiness that comes from the loss. Depressed feelings are common when mourning but can become problematic if they continue without end. We heal by internalizing the good of what we had and by ridding ourselves of the hurt. Depression, in the words of saints, is the dark night of the soul. Lucky for most of us, the sun rises the next day.

Acceptance

At its root, acceptance is a spiritual process. As the final stage of the grieving process it's not only about accepting the bad in your life or resolving your grief; it's about self-growth and assuming your fate with honor.

That means you may have to accept that the man you married fell out of love with you or that your life hasn't followed the path you thought it would. What makes us who we are is not what happens to us but how we deal with the cards we are dealt. Acceptance, at a deep level, allows you to embrace life with less anger and more freedom.

Whatever your spiritual affiliation may be, acceptance is the universal door to moving forward. Reaching the point of acceptance isn't always easy, but getting there is a victory. Whether you believe that it was God or fate that had a hand in your divorce, or that bad things simply happen to good people, acceptance is not a passive state; it's actively taking charge of your life and your future.

Remember: Kids grieve, too. Your psychological health will give you the energy to monitor your children as they experience divorce. After all, parents aren't the only ones who grieve; children grieve, too, but they do so differently than adults.

If children aren't prepared to come to terms with the inadequacies of one parent, they may stay in denial for a longer time. Kids need to believe that they can count on their caretakers, and if they are overwhelmed by sadness or anger toward their parents, it can lead to a deteriorating psychological state, making them depressed, oppositional, or defiant. Often, grieving occurs more actively when they're older and they come to terms with the parent who abandoned or suffocated them.

The Long and Short of It

Now that you've learned about the stages of grief, let's take a look at problem solving. Spiritual traditions teach us that there are two ways to deal with a difficult problem: the long, short way or the short, long way.

You take the short, long way when you want to sidestep a problem. You want to move past the issue quickly, and you believe you won't have to deal with it. When it comes to divorce, this means that you don't want to accept your grief or handle your problems: you want to short-circuit the whole process and pretend you're fine.

This almost always backfires. It just takes longer if you cut corners. You are going to grieve and feel angry. You are going to be in some denial and may even be depressed. Eventually, you'll experience acceptance. It's a process.

Taking the long, short way means that you'll deal with your emotions appropriately. If you're sad, you're sad. If you're angry, you're angry. If you're in a bargaining stage—for good or for bad—you bargain. This process is organic. If you do it right, you'll come out fine.

While you continue to live your life for the sake of your kids or your work, this period is the bruise that's healing. Make sure you care for it tenderly, whether by surrounding yourself with loving family and friends, helpful therapists, or doctors who will monitor your progress. Don't underestimate the value of being heard by those who will listen. Sharing is human, and voicing your emotions is therapeutic. While your community can do wonders, keep in mind that, in extreme cases, medication may also be useful.

A year or two from now, you don't want to be still bargaining, feeling anger, or struggling with depression. The truth is, your marriage didn't work. Maybe you can't stand him. Maybe you can't get along with her. In the end, it doesn't really matter because you have a life to live and children to raise. You are going to make the best of it. That's acceptance.

Regression: When Adults Act Like Children

The terrible irony of divorce is that the moment you feel most pressured and least able to act rationally is the very moment you have to step up, see the big picture, and make sound choices for yourself and your kids. It takes strength and level-headedness to keep an argument behind closed doors or to refrain from using the legal system as a means for revenge. It's also hard to think clearly when you're grieving.

Regression is a psychological term describing how people can backslide to an earlier state of functioning. It's generally not a good thing. During a divorce, normally healthy, rational people often become more anxious, despondent, angry, manipulative, greedy, or helpless. At times, they may be all of those things.

Regression wields a powerful influence because it affects the way people feel and behave. Sadness, lack of energy, over-worrying, anger, antisocial behavior, and even elation (for those who feel liberated by their divorce) can be signs of regression.

To make regression more understandable, let's look first at this phenomenon in children. Sometimes, a toddler who is potty trained starts to soil his bed again. Or a school-aged child starts sucking her thumb after she had given it up three years ago. Or a teen knocks on the door and wants to hang out in your bed, the last thing he would have done six months before the divorce. These are all signs of regression. Each child, under stress, regresses to an earlier stage of development. It's a natural response when their normal security blanket is removed.

Typically, a child will bounce back from these momentary relapses. For example, the teen who comes into your room at night for comfort will probably return to his normal sleep habits in a few days. This is fluidity—individuals who are healthy often move in and out of regressive states. Regression becomes a problem only when a person gets stuck—when the child who was potty trained no longer is.

Like children, adults also regress. As we mentioned, you may feel more needy, depressed, or angry than usual. You may find yourself acting more immature. Everyone has a different temperament. Some people are naturally more anxious, or more suspicious, or more egocentric than others. Then there are those who are genuinely kind, generous, and centered without any obvious issues. When affected by stress, regression causes pre-existing traits to amplify. Your mind misbehaves, and when it does, it's easier to make bad mistakes. This chart shows how stress can affect the way you feel.

The Effects of Regression

Normal		Regressed
Mild Anxiety	→	Panic Attacks
Dependent	→	Helpless
Passive	→	Immobilized
Irritable	→	Rage Attacks
Suspicious	→	Paranoid
Self-Centered	→	Completely Self-Absorbed
Selfish	→	Acts without Conscience
Moody	→	Emotionally Unstable
Organized	→	Compulsive

The stress of divorce can lead to many sleepless nights. The following examples demonstrate a range of behavior for people experiencing regression, from a temporary case of simple anxiety to what it looks like when someone becomes disabled by his or her circumstances.

EXAMPLE
Mel's Sleepless Night

Mel just heard from his attorney that his wife is challenging their custody agreement again. He goes to bed that night and finds himself tossing and turning. He thinks, "I don't know what to do. Here she goes again! This is going to cost so much money and the poor kids."

When Mel wakes the next morning, he calls his attorney.

"I have all these worries," he says. After their conversation, Mel feels reassured. The next night, Mel sleeps better.

"From the Couch"

Mel's experience is an example of normal, transient regression. For one night, he feels helpless and immobilized. He's probably a bit insecure, even when he's at his best, and the news of a new legal battle provokes this reaction. Consulting with his attorney, however, gives Mel the confidence he needs to move forward and to return to a healthy mindset. His experience is common, and it's no big deal.

EXAMPLE
Jerry's Endless Night

Just like Mel, Jerry just heard from his attorney that his wife is challenging their custody agreement again. He goes to bed that night and finds himself tossing and turning, wondering what he's going to do.

"Here she goes again! This is going to cost so much money and the poor kids."

When Jerry wakes the next morning, he calls his attorney to discuss the matter. "I have all these worries," he says.

After their conversation, he has trouble feeling reassured. Jerry is preoccupied, exhausted, and he can't stop his anxiety. His helplessness doesn't go away, leading to more sleepless nights.

"From the Couch"

Unlike Mel, Jerry can't be reassured. He has regressed, and lacks (at least for now) the fluidity that is essential for healthy functioning. But Jerry is not alone. Everyone who goes through a divorce has periods of regression. These are not happy moments but that's to be expected.

Perspective, however, can help you take charge of your thought process when it begins to cloud. During these times, it's especially important to remember that just because you're needy, angry, or bitter it doesn't give you license to do something that will hurt your kids.

How you feel is less important than what you do. With that in mind, let's look at how regression affects judgment. Most of you will probably identify with at least one of these examples. The pressures of divorce can lead to self-destructive behavior, and that's not good for you or your children.

EXAMPLE
Watch the Road

Imagine driving along the highway and thinking, "She doesn't love me anymore." "What's going to happen to me?" "Should I get a new lawyer? Maybe there's something wrong with the one I have."

The inner voices continue. "I can't stand him; he's so selfish." "Nobody is calling me back!" "What's going to happen to my children?"

As the voices grow louder and the worries increase, you become more distracted and overwrought. Your anxiety begins to impair your ability to drive safely. You don't even notice that you just went through a red light.

"From the Couch"

Let's agree that it's good to be alive! You don't want to be regressing while you drive because if your attention wanders it can be deadly. You can control unwanted distractions and be safe.

Did You Know?

In 1970, the National Center for Health Statistics published some scary data on car accidents and marital status. They found that the fatality rate was higher for divorced men and women of all races than for those widowed, married, or single. In fact, on average, the death rate was 2.5 times higher for divorced individuals than for married folks.

Even with the advent of seat belts, these statistics are revealing.

EXAMPLES
Old Habits Die Hard

Bo's wife has left him and he's feeling despondent; he's not sure how he's going to make ends meet. All of a sudden, Bo finds himself with a cigarette in his mouth. His father died of emphysema ten years ago and until this moment, he hasn't touched a single one. The stress of divorce has pushed him to seek the comfort he thinks a cigarette can provide, even though he knows it can kill him.

Comfort Food and Drink

Shereen is living alone and just went on a date with an interesting guy. Surprisingly, he tells Shereen that he doesn't want to see her again. She returns home, alone and rejected. Her kids are sleeping upstairs. The babysitter goes home. Shereen rarely drinks, but half a bottle of wine goes pretty fast. And she's almost finished with a pint of ice-cream.

"From the Couch"

Emotional instability and helplessness are common precursors to resuming bad habits. Data from 2005 to 2007 showed almost twice as many divorced and separated men and women smoking (30.6 percent) than their married counterparts (16.2 percent) (Schoenborn and Adams, 2010). You probably already know that the life expectancy of a chronic smoker is ten years shorter than that of a non-smoker (Kaufman, 2004). Since your kids need you alive and well, this fact is as precious as the statistic on car accidents.

Overeating and drinking are also common. Schoenborn and Adams found that obesity was more prevalent and healthy weight less prevalent among divorced and separated women than among married women. Heavy drinking was also more evident among divorced and separated people.

If smoking and drinking were your coping mechanisms in the past, you may be tempted to succumb to those comfort zones during a divorce. But you don't have to. You can choose healthier behavior. After all, the best mistake is the one you don't make.

Character Traps
How to Handle a (Very) Difficult Ex

It's one thing to make occasional mistakes. It's *destructive* to chronically repeat them. We all know that people under stress are prone to lapses in judgment. When hurt by a series of events that divorce can bring, some react in ways that cause more lasting damage than a simple mistake or two. When people become stuck in a cycle of regressive behavior, they perpetuate conflict, often based on distorted facts that may not be true at all.

Divorcing couples can create a narrative of their experience, casting themselves and others in roles that offer certainty, understanding, and cogency to life. It's convenient when we can justify what's happening; for example, "I'm divorced because he was a jerk" (as if you had nothing to do with it), or "we broke up because she only cared about money" (as if you were never preoccupied with your work). But life is more subtle and complicated than these stories admit.

Walk in the other person's shoes for just ten minutes and the narrative will change completely. You might ask, "Why should I care how real these stories are? They make me feel better." Maybe they do, temporarily, at least, but by getting stuck in a maladaptive narrative— what I call a *character trap*—you make it harder to move forward because you're living in the past and deceiving yourself, as well.

Because the stress of divorce doesn't let up, people frequently get trapped in their regressive behavior, which can manifest itself as one of ten different versions of a character trap. Each narrative depicts someone telling herself about who she is and who her ex is. Is he really the bad guy? Or, is she exaggerating? These stories are dramatic and, while they carry nuggets of truth, they are less than complete.

Ten Common Character Traps

The Archaeologist	The Adolescent
The Denier/The Pleaser	The Narcissist
The Melancholic	The Avenger
The Victim	The Control Freak
The Addict	The Paranoid

Remember, a character in a play tells only his part of the story; he rarely has perspective on what the play is all about.

We're not talking about personality disorders. While two of the character traps (the Narcissist and the Paranoid) bear identical names to known psychiatric conditions, we are moving away from those official labels for a specific reason. Personality disorders are enduring styles of behaving that precede an event, like divorce, by years. A character trap, on the other hand, describes a condition that is often stress-induced and lasts throughout the divorce and not long after.

See if any of the following profiles fit you or your ex. Any one at any time may demonstrate aspects of these character traps. Someone may act like a Victim and display Avenger or Paranoid characteristics as well. The general categories (helpless, selfish, and angry) may also overlap, depending on the person and the situation.

With each of these character traps we will suggest strategies for coping with the described behavior, especially if your ex is filling the profile. In *The Intelligent Divorce—Book Three*, we will be delving much deeper into what happens when your ex is struggling with one of these character traps. When that occurs, you may very well need assistance in the form of counseling or therapy.

For now, let's concentrate on three essential concepts: perspective, limits, and boundaries. Perspective will help you identify the character trap and how it manifests itself in you or your ex's thinking and behavior. Next, you have to set limits on what behavior you will not accept. That will dictate what boundaries you need to maintain in order to optimize a working relationship with your ex-husband or wife. If you are able to properly assess the situation, set good limits, and maintain clear boundaries then you can be open to a more friendly relationship. We hope these tips will help you find your balance.

HELPLESS CHARACTER TRAPS
The Archaeologist

How It Works: You earnestly want to know what went wrong with your marriage. You mobilize your anxiety to comprehend what happened to you and your family. Unconsciously, archaeologists believe they have more control than they really do. They may feel the need to understand the past in order to "get her back" or "make things right." This is similar to the bargaining stage in Elisabeth Kübler-Ross's model on grief, and it's equally counterproductive.

Archaeologists never quite find what they're looking for. They keep digging and digging, but they still have trouble calming their thoughts. Their problem is similar to what Freud called the *repetition compulsion*, the need for the mind to re-engage traumas in order to somehow gain mastery over them. This rarely works. It usually adds to the obsession and creates more phony archaeology.

If You Are an Archaeologist: Your inability to get to the bottom of things immobilizes you. You feel worse, more anxious, and less decisive. You become obsessive about what went wrong and what you could have done differently. These thoughts are endless, and you feel like you are digging into a bottomless pit.

If Your Ex Is an Archaologist: When your ex-husband is an archaeologist, he is ruminating about everything. He can't help but think about what went wrong, what you did wrong, what he could've done better, and what is going to happen to the children. He is overwhelmed with these obsessions. There's no end to it.

With perspective, you will understand that he is really suffering, but if it continues it will be destructive to everyone. A person who is not getting over the divorce is still grieving and stuck in the bargaining stage without moving on.

Sasha's Story

This divorce has been really hard. When we were younger, Carlos was my whole world. I know we had grown distant, that things weren't as great as they had been, but I didn't think we were headed for divorce. Ever since he uttered that word, my mind has been racing. I want to know where I failed. I feel like some country singer lamenting about her life. But for me, it is real, and I can't seem to stop. I wish I could just let all of this go.

Sasha, age 43

What You Can Do: Sometimes, you have to accept that your marriage wasn't meant to be and break away from the cyclical narrative that is holding you back. You must abandon this obsessive project, either through your own will or with the help of a psychotherapist. Acknowledging that you have no control over the past and that it's time to move on is essential to regaining your freedom.

When it's your ex who is the archaologist, your first approach may be to join him in his suffering (if he lets you in), saying things like, "I understand what you're going through and I'm sorry that I've contributed to it, but you're going to have to move on." Encourage him to get help. Point out that all his ruminations only agitate the kids and everyone else.

Your kids can probably see how much their father is preoccupied with his pain. They may be overly nice to him or they may feel burdened by the fact that their father can't get over the divorce. With that in mind, and remembering that children want to look up to their parents, the limits you set with an archaologist are important.

At some point, you have to be firm. Let him know by telling him: "You can't keep doing this." "It's upsetting the kids." "You're never going to get past this if you don't get help." You may even offer to go to therapy with him at first in order to move things along. At some point you may have to become harder and even angry because, by indulging in archaological behavior, your ex is slowing down the process for everybody, particularly the kids. It may feel cruel to be stern, but sometimes it's required because they just don't get it.

The Pleaser

How It Works: A pleaser is locked into an infantile hope that if he says or does the right thing, everything will be okay. The pleaser can't believe the marriage is over and hopes beyond hope that the whole thing will work out.

If You Are a Pleaser: You're someone who hopes for the best. You put off tough decisions and minimize your ex's manipulation.

Believing that "it's not as bad as it looks" reduces your anxiety. You're always willing to compromise, even when you shouldn't.

This strategy of giving in rarely works. It's vital that you know what you need and make healthy demands. Pleasers are often stepped on, always to their own detriment. Your ex will keep upping the ante, getting more out of you. This will set a bad example for your kids.

The mind is not immune to gaming itself. When you are under stress and have a lot on your plate, you can be convinced to ignore a problem that needs attention.

Pleasers have trouble seeing beyond the characters they have chosen for themselves and their ex to play, and it's almost impossible to overcome their mind games without outside help.

If Your Ex Is a Pleaser: When dealing with an ex-spouse who is a pleaser, your life looks easy. He'll agree with what you want, go into therapy with you, and concede with many, if not all, of your demands. It may not even feel like it's in your best

Ari's Story

We were in therapy, working on our marriage. My wife had engaged in an ongoing affair and had two casual affairs on the side. She wasn't serious about our marriage and she knew it, but I was a stable provider and she was conniving. She wanted to position herself so she would come out of a divorce okay. When her lover finally decided to leave his marriage, it was the end of mine. It was also the end of my denial. In some strange way, this guy did me a favor. I finally woke up.

Ari, age 36

interest to do anything about a pleaser because after all, he is pleasing you, but nothing can be further from the truth. The Pleaser demonstrates a terrible role model for your children and encourages you to be self-centered and boorish. Neither of these positions is pleasant for your children to see.

What You Can Do: If you are the pleaser, you are going to have to confront the fact that he no longer loves you and that you cannot make him love you by doing whatever he wants. A psychotherapist would invite you to look at your fear and point out that you are probably more capable than you think. Pleasers placate others out of fear and out of habit. With that in mind, it may be time to try something else.

If your ex is the pleaser, the first step would be to join him in his suffering. Tell him that "You can't just lie down and let people walk all over you. You're not moving on, and it's not good for the kids."

If a pleaser continues for too long, he'll eventually feel like a Victim and build up enough data points to become self-righteous and angry. Soon enough you'll hear things like, "Look what I did for you and how you paid me back." Trust me; you don't want to deal with a victim mentality. Set limits by being sharp and direct. "Stop trying to please everyone." You may consider putting your children in therapy because they could be dealing with a very passive person, which is not healthy for their mental growth.

If you succeed in setting limits you may end up with an ex spouse who sees that a more effective relationship is about respect, not helplessness. He may come to see that his tendency to please made him weak in the marriage but that he doesn't have to continue that anymore. He may develop a stronger center that's good for the children and for you, too.

Many people finally find their voice in the divorce after feeling stifled in marriage.

The Melancholic

How It Works: No matter what you're facing, you feel a certain relief when you're able to say, "I just can't deal with this; let me sleep." It's a convenient way to avoid the issue and hope it's gone when you wake up. Melancholics tend to experience themselves as victims whose sadness has enveloped them, so much so that it becomes who they are.

If You Are a Melancholic: When grief turns into melancholia and then to depression, you're not an effective advocate for yourself or for your kids. You are in a position to be exploited, and your kids will notice and feel demoralized. They may feel like they need to pick up the pieces for you and assume the parent role. Their innocence must be protected, and if you're depressed and unable to be strong for your kids, you should seek treatment.

If Your Ex Is a Melancholic: Your ex-spouse may have a medical diagnosis that is difficult to overcome. Grief that doesn't get resolved can descend into depression, which is characterized by low energy, injured self-esteem, staying in bed, poor decision making, self-recrimination, negative thoughts about the future, and even, at times, self-destructive and suicidal behaviors. The key here is to understand that this person must be mobilized to do something, because whether it is unresolved grief or more serious depression, she won't be able to properly take care of the children.

The melancholic perspective is filled with misplaced judgment and anger. A melancholic won't be setting a good example for the kids and may sleep instead of taking care of important things. The first step is to join with her if you can and insist that she must do something for the sake of the kids. Once again, you can go with her for the first therapy session to get the ball rolling. This is good for children.

Regina's Story

My life has changed since I divorced. I can't quite put one foot in front of the other. Thank God I have three healthy kids who take care of the house and who are self-starters. I don't even have to tell them to do their homework. I also have a tough attorney who does the thinking for me.

Honestly, I don't know if I'm ever going to get over this.

Regina, age 30

What You Can Do: If you suspect that you are a melancholic, learn more about the diagnosis of depression. You may have such low motivation that you are barely invested in your kids or in yourself. Those who care about you, like a parent, a friend, or even a particularly compassionate ex, may encourage you to see a doctor. Follow that advice. If you are feeling suicidal or just don't "want to deal with another day," then your need for help is urgent. With proper care, you should get better.

If your ex is the melancholic, partial limits may need to be set, which seems paradoxical because who wants to be sharp with someone who is suffering? But you are responsible for your children's well-being and when your ex-wife has her time with the children she needs to be on top of her game.

In worst-case scenarios, you may have to enlist the help of outside authorities. First, you might threaten to take action if she doesn't get help. Then, you document just how dysfunctional she may be, and, finally, you may be forced to seek modifications to your custody agreement.

Depressed people can do terrible things when in despair, so if it has reached a low point, you will need excellent advice. At the end of the day, the melancholic may be remarkably responsive to proper treatments. I've seen countless patients turn around with good therapy and medication. Your relationship with her may well open up if it's handled well. This is not a hopeless situation, but it can be if it's allowed to linger.

The Victim

How It Works: You're hurt, so you're careful to protect yourself—often at all costs, which means in many cases your own children can be the real victims.

If You Are a Victim: You take the desire to protect yourself to the extreme. For example, you blame your ex for everything that's happened. Or you feel justified in inflicting damage on him because he hurt you. You may descend into helplessness because you believe you have no control over your life.

This narrative is common, especially for the person who has been left. We all know what it's like to feel like a victim. You feel like whatever you may have done wrong in life or in the marriage, you didn't deserve "this." You didn't deserve the affair or him taking all the money. You didn't deserve her saying, after many years of marriage, "I never really loved you." Of course you feel like a victim. How else can you feel? Just be careful not to stay there for too long.

If Your Ex Is a Victim: You are going to be blamed for everything. A victim not only feels bad about her life; she believes she's innocent and has been hurt by you. You may have left the marriage because you were suffering or because she was wrong for you; it doesn't matter. She believes that the divorce is entirely your fault and no matter what you do, you'll be blamed for everything. You are going to have to accept this without overreacting.

Victims are remarkably good at triggering you to respond aggressively, only to reinforce their sense of being victimized. If you have a temper, a nasty tongue, or a history of being cruel to her, it will make this project that much harder because you have to curb your own reactions in order to begin to work with her. The approach here is to begin once again by joining your ex-wife; understand that you will be blamed, but ignore it for now and remember that you are there for your children.

Lilly's Story

Paul constantly second-guessed me. Whether it was the food I made, the way I raised the children, or even how the kids did in school; nothing was ever right and everything was always my fault.

When Paul left me for our old friend, Meg, I couldn't help but feel like a victim. After Paul moved out, I began leaning on my nine-year-old daughter, Lily. I kept seeking her company, even when she wanted to play with her friends. I told her too much about her dad, and I could feel her pulling away from me, for her own protection. I was a basket case.

Lilly, age 38

What You Can Do: If you assume the role of the victim, be aware of a deep feeling of gratification that you are right and she is wrong. While this may be true, holding the victim position will thwart your ability to move forward and enjoy the precious years ahead of you. Protecting yourself from a malignant ex-spouse is commendable but refrain from nursing non-productive anger that may never really abate.

If your ex is the victim, you need to tell her, "We can't keep going to court and we can't be bad-mouthing each other in front of the children." Sometimes, the less regressed part of the victim can engage you and work on holding back her anger. When this moment presents itself, it may be useful to diffuse some of the actions of the victim.

Finally, if she is completely attached to victim status, you will have very little opportunity for a productive discussion and you will have to work within the limits she has created by her behavior. All good conversation will have to happen between third parties, and a solid parenting plan that is sanctioned by the court will have to suffice. Stick to every detail and don't give her more room for her self-righteousness. It will only backfire on the kids and on you. Despite the fact that this can be an impossible person, you have free time away from her and you can be happy in other settings.

SELFISH CHARACTER TRAPS
The Addict

How It Works: Addiction is physiological and psychological. The body craves the high or the numbing dependency that a particular drug provides. The soul craves respite from life's pressures. Addicts abuse substances (or activities) to escape the harsh realities of life brought on by a divorce.

There are many addictions, including sex addiction, computer addiction, and the more classic drug and alcohol addictions. Addicts always want more; what they have is never enough. They think morning, noon, and night about their object or activity of desire.

In Alcoholics Anonymous, this is called "stinking thinking." Your mind games itself into believing that you can handle more than you can, which leads you to neglect your work, your children, and your relationships. Your addiction comes first; it's your secret life and your way of finding pleasure in a world that can feel so empty. There are healthier ways to find rest. If you're an addict, get help.

If You Are An Addict: You're not facing reality, and you're subjecting your body, your mind, and your family to dangerous behavior. You may feel like you're in control, but addicts never

---

Kate's Story

When my husband ran off to figure out his mid-life crisis, I was left with two young boys and a mountain of bills. My neighbor was kind of a drunk, but she was friendly, and I needed a shoulder to cry on sometimes. Soon enough, I found myself not only drinking and smoking; I was developing a gambling habit, hoping to hit it big and solve my financial problems. I kept telling myself it was my husband's fault and I had to win big for my boys. I was an idiot. When I finally realized my gambling had turned into a full-blown addiction, it was already too late. I lost my kids to the state and now I'm trying to clean myself up and get them back.

Kate, age 40

are. Addiction makes you feel better in the moment, and it's a crutch you've come to rely upon.

If Your Ex Is An Addict: The addict desperately wants to be satisfied, like an itch always needing to be scratched. He will fool himself into thinking that he's fine or convince you that it's all in the past. For the true addict, that is rarely the case. They employ rationalization, minimizing, and blaming better than anyone I've ever seen. Addicts want their drug (whatever form it takes) and will justify their behavior in order to get what they want.

It's not always unconscious; sometimes they know full well that they're manipulating you. For instance, he'll tell you that he won't smoke marijuana around the kids, but he already plans on sneaking a few hits of a joint when he thinks the kids are sleeping (despite swearing to you, the attorney, and the judge that he won't.) Or they may unconsciously fool themselves, believing that they are going to refrain, but then don't.

"What's the problem with a few beers? Nobody needs to know."

"I've only lost $100 tonight playing poker; it's my loss; and who cares?"

"What's the big deal about internet pornography? I'm a man, and it's my private life, nobody needs to know." (No one except his 12-year-old daughter, who sees everything on the computer, after he passes out on the couch.)

What You Can Do: If you are the addict, you will be convincing yourself that everyone is over reacting. Addicts live in denial and usually only get help when they have really hit bottom. Don't wait. Get a consultation with an addiction counselor or go to an AA meeting (Alcoholics Anonymous) in your community. Seeing others like yourself may motivate you to get the help that you desperately need.

When dealing with and ex who has an addiction, you must set limits. ALANON, among many other support groups, can help you to do this. You have to assume that the addict is not telling the truth and he needs to know there will be real consequences if he transgresses. If a person gambles away his money or uses drugs privately, you have little say: that's his problem. However, when it spills over into his time with the children and his responsibilities, you have to put your foot down. If he gets violent under the influence, putting your foot down means getting law enforcement involved.

Judges do not take kindly to a parent with a DWI; nor do they respond well to hearing that a parent smelled of alcohol when returning a child, or that he failed to pay child support after losing thousands on internet gambling. And physical assault or verbal abuse while under the influence may lead to an order of protection or jail time. Addictions are costly in many ways.

Addictions have to be dealt with dispassionately. He'll have to get treatment, which should include a support group, whether it is Alcoholics Anonymous, Gamblers Anonymous, Narcotics Anonymous, or Sex Addicts Anonymous. These groups will help addicts to face reality. This is a very difficult story to live, but you can effect real change with a sober assessment of your ex-spouse. Learn about what she's dealing with and how to keep it under control, both for her safety and for your children's.

If your ex-spouse gets to the other side of addiction, he may be a very different man than the one you had to leave. Down the road, and with hard work, you may just achieve a more open dialogue with your now sober ex-husband. This is the best possible outcome for everyone.

The Adolescent

How It Works: After years of a miserable marriage, you're finally free and having a good time. After all, everyone deserves some happiness, right?

If You Are An Adolescent: You're so preoccupied with your pleasure that you don't take proper care of your children. You become self-centered and your kids feel abandoned. There's nothing inherently wrong with feeling free; problems arise when you focus solely on your happiness and lose your sense of parental responsibility.

The first weeks or months of a breakup may be devastating. Even though you have lost the important structures of marriage and family that took years to build, the change can suddenly be exhilarating. Freedom is alluring: staying out all hours of the night, drinking excessively, sleeping with multiple partners. These actions are remnants of a younger, more irresponsible mindset. People who were responsible in their marriage can regress to an almost unrecognizable state of recklessness.

I've seen too many parents make the same mistake. They bring a boyfriend or girlfriend home and into their bedroom way before their kids could possibly be ready. Or some forget that it's more important to help their kids with homework instead of surfing internet dating sites. Or they become so obsessed with losing weight and looking their best that their kids never see them.

If Your Ex Is An Adolescent: Your ex may not have been the most mature person when you married him, but now that he is free, he's really indulging in being a teen despite his adult responsibilities.

Typical behavior of an ex who is an adolescent includes missing appointments, exposing the kids to new girlfriends or boyfriends too quickly, and, most dangerous, putting their needs before the needs of the children. Like many teenagers, your ex-spouse can start acting rather self-centered. She feels like she did her part and now she is liberated, free to do whatever feels right.

Pat's Story

My sister, Christy, was married to this jerk for years. He just wasn't nice to her. He was always critical and telling her she wasn't good enough. When he left, Christy was devastated.

Suddenly, just two months after the breakup, Christy seemed happier than ever. She signed up on a few dating websites and she started going out most nights. She kept seeing some of the same guys, and adding new dates as well.

It's like Christy became a new woman. I saw this confidence about her. She realized that there are men who like and accept her for who she is.

It seems liberating. She still takes good care of her teenagers and manages her fun discreetly. She's divorced, but she's happy as can be!

Pat, age 56

What You Can Do: You know you are acting like an adolescent if your divorce is becoming a fun excuse for going out all the time and exploiting your new lease on life at the expense of your children. If that's the case, get with the program and be there for your kids!

If you find yourself getting annoyed with your ex because she wants you to act like an adult, pay attention! There may be some truth to her claim. Take a deep breath; give up some dates, drinking with your pals, and your special "away time," and be the father your children need right now. There will be plenty of time for fun in the coming years.

When your ex behaves like an adolescent it can be exactly like dealing with another teenager. When adults act this way, especially when there are kids in the mix, you have to set limits, but mostly for your own sanity. Promise yourself that you're going to act responsibly and at the same time, hold your ex accountable for his behavior.

Despite the aggravation, you must deal with this intelligently because of your kids. You have resources in court and with attorneys. You can also attempt to understand his psychological mindset, but counsel him that his kids come first and point out that he has private time alone to do what he wants.

In the end, you may be surprised. People can step up when they don't feel attacked. If it doesn't work out and he continues to show gross negligence, a judge may limit his access to the children. Under these circumstances, maybe he'll wake up, and maybe he won't.

The Narcissist

How It Works: The word "narcissist" is derived from the Greek myth of Narcissus, a youth who couldn't stop staring at his own image in a pond. He lost interest in food, drink, and self-care, and so he died. His story illustrates the emptiness and incessant personal preoccupation that characterizes the narcissistic character trap. Individuals who assume this role are manipulative, self-important know-it-alls. They think only about what's in their best interest. Often, they are unaware of how selfish they are, even when it comes to their kids.

If You Are a Narcissist: You were probably in an unhappy marriage and you feel best watching out for yourself. You will lie and manipulate, but look good in the process. If you've been injured, even a slight amount, you'll offer no forgiveness and you'll be sure your ex knows it. Eventually, she will catch on and never trust you again. You become more and more shallow and have learned little from the marriage or the divorce. You will probably continue to make mistakes in future relationships. Your children will probably figure out your game when they get older.

If Your Ex Is a Narcissist: Most narcissists have an unusual ability or trait; they may be beautiful, handsome, brilliant, or influential or have some incredible artistic talent. If you married a narcissist, he or she probably led you to believe that you really counted. Unfortunately, the only people narcissists care about are those who make them feel good in the moment and

Cynthia's Story

Sam was handsome, charismatic, and he made a good living. Once we had kids, the excitement of our relationship wore off. He was always looking to have a good time, and it became clear that he was no longer interested in me. At some point, I started to feel like an accessory raising his kids.

When we divorced, it was as if there was never any love in the first place. He claimed I never worked and that I wasn't entitled to his money. It was like I was put out with the trash. It's going to take some time to get over this. Was this love ever real?

Cynthia, Age 32

who can help them climb the ladder. Narcissists are preoccupied with the endgame—what's in it for them. Fair is not part of their emotional vocabulary.

Interestingly, as narcissists age and are no longer as beautiful, handsome, alluring, or capable as they once were, they often see themselves with more objectivity. When they realize that they've been manipulative their whole lives and how they've filled their world with shallow relationships, some of them actually attempt to make things right. They may not work it out with you—it's probably too late for that—but when narcissists finally figure it out, it's a good thing for everyone else.

If your ex was always a narcissist, you have to first accept that he will never love you and may never have really loved you. You are an object rather than the mother of his kids. And all your pain and upset will change nothing.

I recommend that you consult a therapist because dealing with an ex in the narcissistic range can make you crazy. They always think they are right even as they exploit you or neglect the kids. Narcissists are very connected to how they are perceived by others and it will upset you to see how he is able to garner so much sympathy while treating you so badly. You will have to learn to be dispassionate in your dealings with him, which is much easier said than done.

A note of caution: thus far, we've spoken only about the "Narcissist Light"—the ex who never loved you, but only himself. But there is a darker side to narcissism, and it surrounds something most people don't understand: the narcissistic injury. If you take a self-righteous person who sees no flaws within herself and you hurt her at her core, the results can be disastrous. She'll never forgive you and she'll attempt to cut you out of her life and your kids' lives. If you think you're doing this to your family, get help. If you're on the other end of this emotional abuse, you also need serious help.

What You Can Do: And how can you tell whether you're suffering from this character trap? Given that narcissists have precious little insight about themselves, you probably aren't. If you think only—and I mean *only*—about what's in this divorce for you, or if you're preoccupied with having your friends and family see you as the shining star in this process, then it's time to raise an eyebrow at your behavior.

Are you using your intelligence to convince yourself that you're thinking about others when you're not? In your heart of hearts, do you see your ex as someone to "manage" rather than as the person you once loved or the mother (or father) of your children? If so, it's time to stop gazing at your image and deal honestly with your family.

ANGRY CHARACTER TRAPS
The Avenger

How It Works: You've been wronged, and you want to set the record straight. At best, there is something cynical about the avenger—and that's the healthy avenger who simply wants to hurt because he feels victimized. It may not be a nice thing, but at least he's conscious of his actions. The unhealthy avenger is even more stuck in his character role, believing that his misbehavior is correct. He feels no guilt, and is self-righteous. This personality is one of the toughest character traps in the divorce system. He or she consumes a vast majority of legal, monetary, and psychotherapeutic resources.

If You Are An Avenger: Revenge may be the motivating force behind the most important decisions in your life. For the sake of your kids, you will need to get along with your ex for years to come. If your children are dragged into endless and unnecessary battles, they can be easily damaged.

Avengers and victims are closely related. They're all about getting even and hurting their ex because he or she deserves it. To do this, they will use any means at their disposal, whether poisoning their children against the ex, ruining the ex's reputation in front of their friends, hiding money that rightfully belongs to the ex, or using the legal system as a bludgeon. Avengers see problems as outside of themselves.

Typical avenger behavior might include calling Child Protective Services when you know your ex-husband or wife hasn't abused the kids, calling the police when you know your ex hasn't been threatening, or obtaining an order of protection simply because you want leverage in front of the judge.

Do you see yourself in any of this described behavior?

If you are about to lose control and feel that you may hurt someone, get immediate help. In a moment of regressed anger or despair, some people do the unthinkable. If you hurt someone you love or once loved, there is no turning back.

If Your Ex Is An Avenger: There are some people who are so hurt or psychologically disordered that they believe they are entitled to abuse the system and their ex even when an objective observer would disagree. In pedestrian terms, we view people like this as crazy, and it's amazing what havoc they can wreak on the system.

Crazy or not, lawyers must still file and answer motions, police must still respond to calls, Child Protective Services must still document complaints, and judges must still make life-altering decisions. All of this is harder when you are dealing with someone who believes his or her own lies. Consider how difficult it is for a psychiatrist to perform a custody evaluation when he can't untangle truth from fiction.

If you are certain that your ex is an avenger, be wary, very wary. She may make false accusations to gain leverage over you. And kidnapping and violence does sometimes occur when an ex is particularly disturbed. Protect yourself and your children. Work closely with your lawyer and document everything.

If you are worried about violence or abduction, your ex may be monitored by the court and you may be granted an order of protection. If there is a kidnapping risk, for instance, a judge can limit vitiation or have a passport taken out of his possession.

Marcus's Story

My ex-wife always had a short fuse but it was never a big deal until I filed for divorce. It was as if she couldn't accept the fact that I had the nerve to actually say no to her because I wanted to better my life and our children's, too. That's when her temper became full blown. She started hitting me, throwing things, and scaring the kids. It wasn't long before she began lying to the police about me hitting her. My lawyer had a tough time getting things straightened out. Years later, I still don't feel completely safe when she's around.

Marcus, Age 49

What You Can Do: A successful divorce means protecting the innocence of your children. Punishing your ex for the sake of revenge will hurt your children, and you may get yourself into legal trouble while doing so. For instance, keep in mind that there are consequences for false reporting, and not everyone successfully cheats the system. As an example of how serious the repercussions may be, take a look at one small piece of the State of Florida's law on false reporting of child abuse, neglect, or abandonment:

> *"A person who knowingly and willfully makes a false report of child abuse, abandonment, or neglect, or who advises another to make a false report, is guilty of a felony of the third degree."* (2009 Florida Statutes 39.205 & 39.206)

State laws exist to protect children and adults who are in abusive situations. These laws are not meant to be used as weapons in divorce proceedings and judges do not take kindly to the misuse of the system.

The Control Freak

How It Works: The control freak is always ready to fight. He sees the divorce as a battle, one that must be won, no matter what. This person probably contributed to the marriage's demise by always having to have it his way. People who are trapped in this narrative won't engage in productive conversation or negotiate. They're tough, and they stand their ground.

If You Are a Control Freak: You were anxious in your marriage, and now that things are spinning out of control, you're determined to take the reins and prevent something bad from happening. It may not feel good, but it feels like the only thing you can do. You fail to see that there are two sides to most issues, so your ex-husband or wife is going to feel hounded and harassed. As a consequence, you may be left paying costly legal fees, find your children upset with you, and end up stuck in a divorce with irresolvable issues.

Yumi's Story

When my ex filed for divorce, it felt like the rug had been pulled out from underneath me. Even though I knew he was a good man, I never trusted him. I admit that I drove my lawyer crazy and made my kids go through a lot more aggravation than was necessary. Finally, I started seeing a therapist and it ended up saving all of us.

Yumi, Age 42

If Your Ex Is a Control Freak: In the control freak's eyes, you never do anything right. Unfortunately, if this person is wealthy, she's likely to push the legal process battle as far as it will go until she has won all that she can.

What You Can Do: If you are the control freak, it is very unlikely that you will want to change because you are too invested in having it your way. If you are a "nice" control freak, you may work quietly behind the scenes to get everyone on your side. If you have a nastier nature, you may be paying your attorney a lot of money to harass your ex. To give up this role is to allow grief to enter your soul and accept the pain of loss. All the control in the world will not give you what you really want.

When dealing with a control freak, the best strategy is often to stay as collected as possible. At the same time, you must ensure that he or she doesn't take advantage of you. One day, your kids will appreciate that you've made every attempt to provide them with a comfortable, stable life.

The Paranoid

How It Works: Paranoia is more common than people think. Most paranoids aren't schizophrenic, manic-depressive, delusional, or hearing voices; they are just suspicious to the extreme and unwilling to change their minds even when presented with new facts.

If You Are Paranoid: You are anxious, but you get some sense of stability out of believing that everyone is against you. Even a broken clock is right twice a day. You aren't dealing with reality. You provoke your ex, find yourself paying enormous attorney bills, unnecessarily involve the police, and cause trauma for everyone.

If Your Ex Is Paranoid: For someone who may already be suspicious, there is a reasonable chance that the stress of divorce will push her into this character trap. This narrative dictates that everyone is out to get her, that there is an ulterior motive to every action, and that the divorce is wrought with manipulation. The paranoid person has lost trust, even in herself. You will need mental health support in order to understand her. You will need legal help if she is proving unreliable or even unstable with the children.

Kevin's Story

As a divorce lawyer, I handle all kinds. But the most difficult type of person is the one who is convinced that the world is out to get him. With someone like that, no matter what I do, it's never enough. I wish I could get those folks to do mandatory therapy.

Kevin, age 50

If your ex is not too severe, inundate her with details about your plans. Sometimes, she will feel reassured for the moment. If she is really severe, you will be suspected and accused of many things. Don't take it too seriously, but do consult your attorney if there are legal ramifications. If things deteriorate, a judge may remove custody because of ongoing paranoia.

What You Can Do: Paranoids feel secure because they "know how the world works" and believe that it's them against everyone else. If you're a true Paranoid, you'll probably want to put down this book because we are asking that you think seriously about the validity of your beliefs. But if you care about your children, you may also consider getting help.

Character Traps:
Assessing Yourself and Your Ex

Please take a look at the charts on the following two pages and assess which character traps, if any, apply to your current situation. There can be considerable overlap, with traits of two or three character traps found in one person. Be honest. No one else needs to see your answers and there is nothing to be embarrassed about. This can give you important insight into how you deal with your children and your ex. It can help you take advantage of therapy so you can avoid overreacting or under reacting when you're faced with important decisions.

Assessing Myself

Circle the word or phrase that best describes your level of identification with the following character traps.

1. **I am an Archaeologist.**
    not at all   a little bit   somewhat   very much   completely

2. **I am a Pleaser.**
    not at all   a little bit   somewhat   very much   completely

3. **I am a Melancholic.**
    not at all   a little bit   somewhat   very much   completely

4. **I am a Victim.**
    not at all   a little bit   somewhat   very much   completely

5. **I am an Addict.**
    not at all   a little bit   somewhat   very much   completely

6. **I am an Adolescent.**
    not at all   a little bit   somewhat   very much   completely

7. **I am a Narcissist.**
    not at all   a little bit   somewhat   very much   completely

8. **I am an Avenger.**
    not at all   a little bit   somewhat   very much   completely

9. **I am a Control Freak.**
    not at all   a little bit   somewhat   very much   completely

10. **I am a Paranoid.**
    not at all   a little bit   somewhat   very much   completely

Assessing My Ex-Spouse

Circle the word or phrase that best describes how your ex-spouse fits the following character traps.

1. **My ex-spouse is an Archaeologist.**
   not at all   a little bit   somewhat   very much   completely

2. **My ex-spouse is a Pleaser.**
   not at all   a little bit   somewhat   very much   completely

3. **My ex-spouse is a Melancholic.**
   not at all   a little bit   somewhat   very much   completely

4. **My ex-spouse is a Victim.**
   not at all   a little bit   somewhat   very much   completely

5. **My ex-spouse is an Addict.**
   not at all   a little bit   somewhat   very much   completely

6. **My ex-spouse is an Adolescent.**
   not at all   a little bit   somewhat   very much   completely

7. **My ex-spouse is a Narcissist.**
   not at all   a little bit   somewhat   very much   completely

8. **My ex-spouse is an Avenger.**
   not at all   a little bit   somewhat   very much   completely

9. **My ex-spouse is a Control Freak.**
   not at all   a little bit   somewhat   very much   completely

10. **My ex-spouse is a Paranoid.**
    not at all   a little bit   somewhat   very much   completely

The Quest for Serenity

You may have answered "not at all," "a little bit," or "somewhat" on a number of these character traps. That's normal. If, however, you find that you identify "very much" or "completely" with one or more of them, you may be more stuck than you think, and it might be time to seek outside support from a caring, objective family member, a clergyman, or a therapist. Ask yourself, "does this strategy really work for my family or me?" Character traps may work in the short run, but eventually they will become damaging to parents and their children.

We close this section with the Serenity Prayer. While it has a long and significant place in the rooms of Alcoholics Anonymous, it's applicable for everyone. Finding your center is finding personal power. Finding that kind of power is the pathway to finding serenity.

Serenity Prayer

*God grant me the serenity to accept
the things I cannot change;
the courage to change
the things I can;
and the wisdom
to know the difference.*

Notes

This space is for you—to remember what's important, to doodle, to make plans ...

CHAPTER 4

Lessons in Freedom

When Adults Act Their Age

Before you wrap your freedom in a gift box we recommend digging deeply once again to examine what happens during the stress of a divorce. While most of you will give ample thought to your actions, you probably won't spend endless hours analyzing the personal history that informs your behavior. That's the work of proper self-analysis, which can be achieved with the help of a therapist or, with effort, on your own. After all, how can you be in charge of your future if you're always reacting to your past?

The ability to be conscious of how you think (also known as *metacognition*) is amazing, and it's not something we do regularly. It comes with practice, and many of the questions we suggest you ask yourself can lead you in that direction.

With that in mind, we hope you now have a better understanding of regression and character traps. You won't get it right every time (who does?) but perspective, insight, and love for your kids will give you the strength you need to save the day.

In this chapter, we will return to the subject of regression and show you how it affects the way you actually think and not just how you feel. This will lead to an examination of triggers. How does your ex-spouse trigger you, and what can you do about it? We will show you how past events in your life make you vulnerable to repeating the same old mistakes; something Freud called the *repetition compulsion*. Finally, you will learn how to take charge of your future by essentially writing a new story for yourself.

But first, let's look at how regression can change the way a person thinks. I call it the *four illusions*. Below are some basic assumptions that get people into trouble. Ask yourself if you or your ex buy into any of these illusions.

Illusion One
A court of law will set the record straight and solve my psychological injuries.

Any matrimonial lawyer will tell you that judges in divorce courts are not your parents. They will not really get to know you, and they won't solve all your psychological problems. You may go into court assuming that they are going to pay attention to all of your stories and the assorted minutiae of your life, but that probably will never happen. The more you try to push yourself on the court the more things can backfire, meaning things may not turn out the way you wanted. It's immature to think judges will do the right thing for you. Sometimes they do and sometimes they don't. Going to court in the first place is taking an enormous risk that they will get it right— according to you.

"He's going to pay. I'll make sure he's never going to be financially comfortable again."

"Wait 'till a judge sees just how passive-aggressive she really is."

"She's so unstable. It'll come out in court and I'll get the kids. I can't wait. It's my due."

Most people consider retribution, justice, and revenge when they divorce. Unfortunately, many consider a court of law as some kind of celestial palace where all wrongs will be righted. This is a classic example of regressive thinking. Most likely, it will come back to bite you. In my experience, you lose a lot of control in the courtroom. You'll rarely find a judge who sees his or her cases with an unbiased, godlike clarity. Assuming that you will prevail is simply naïve.

Illusion Two
My friends and family will understand and help me through this.

Friends and family often disappear during divorce—not physically, but emotionally. What you're going through may be too strange or disturbing, even for those closest to you. It's very easy to feel isolated and alone during this time. You will eventually learn who you can count on. Be open to new people and understand that your support system may not be all that it's cracked up to be.

Ralph's Story

This divorce has revealed who my true friends really are. Those who have come through surprise me, and I'm shocked by those who haven't.

Teddy and I were buddies for 12 years. We met in college. I thought it was nice that our wives got along; they did all their shopping together and we hung out as a group whenever we had the chance. I didn't think their friendship would be the end of mine. I guess Teddy feels like he needs to stay away from me because his wife sided with my ex. I just don't get it.

Ralph, age 32

Don't spend a lot of psychic energy on disappointment. It can be devastating, especially coming from someone you thought would be nice or take care of you. Ruminating endlessly over someone who didn't come through can undermine your recovery.

Jane's Story

I was so close to my mother-in-law. I know it doesn't sound right, but it hurts that she hasn't spoken to me since I divorced her son. After all, she knows how hard it is to live with him. My father-in-law is the same way.

Jane, age 28

During the grieving process, some people will be there for you and some people won't. Adults who care and can spend time with you can diffuse some of your regressive moments. This will help prevent blow-ups with your ex-husband or an angry exchange with your ten-year-old daughter.

A final note of caution about depending on the wrong people: we all know where we can find a ready audience who will, almost certainly, give you attention when it's requested—your children. When you're regressed and disappointed, it's all too easy to turn to them: to spend extra time watching TV; to invite them into bed to snuggle; to share with them how unhappy you are about your life; or, when you're really misbehaving, complaining about their mother or father. As you deal with the disappointment of your divorce, it's essential that you let your kids be kids. Find the adult support that you need.

Illusion Three
I trust my feelings. I'll do the right thing.

In the heat of a divorce, try not to make important decisions when you're experiencing a rush of emotion. Feelings can be like small tsunamis that take control for minutes, hours, or even days. You may be just fine, but then a wave of regret or hurt simply overwhelms you.

Your feelings are real. But the emotional life of divorcing people can be dramatic, sometimes to the extreme. It's part of the deal. The key is not to react in the moment, when you find yourself suddenly scared or boiling over. Feelings like this pass, and there will be time to act from an intelligent position when you are less overwhelmed.

EXAMPLE
Mia Won't Compromise

Mia was angry at her husband, Jonathan, for failing to uphold his part of their custody agreement. He was chronically late returning the kids on Sunday afternoons. Jonathan didn't like Mia's nagging during the marriage, and he hated it during the divorce. Mia decided she was no longer going to abide by his "passive-aggressive bullshit."

Instead of talking to him, reasoning with him, or finding a neutral third party to help them with this issue, Mia went straight to her attorney. She told him that Jonathan was out of control and requested that he file a motion to have the custody arrangement re-assessed.

For $1,500, the motion was filed. In turn, Jonathan had to defend himself. His attorney's bill was $6,000.

They had to take off work to go to court, only to have the judge postpone the date.

It's now five years later, and Mia's divorce has cost her $75,000, money she simply doesn't have. She realizes that she and Jonathan started a process that spun out of control because they were hurt and angry. Looking back Mia wishes she had been a little calmer and talked all this through.

"I'd certainly be richer today."

"From the Couch"

There are legitimate reasons to seek redress through the legal system. It can be a powerful tool. But be careful, because in the hands of someone overwhelmed by emotion, the law can easily become an irrational weapon.

You may think you've moved beyond a challenging series of events and that you've solved some of your problems, and perhaps you have. But just because you think you're right doesn't always mean you are. You trust your feelings but you may have miscalculated the situation.

Regression can distort your perspective. You may think your ex is more dangerous than he or she really is; you may think your kids are having more problems than they actually are; or you may believe that you, yourself, are in danger. This may all be true. But there's also the chance that you're wrong.

When you're in a heightened state of emotion, take a deep breath and ask yourself whether you need to react immediately. You may want to take time to consult with a professional who has dealt with divorce, like a pediatrician, a member of the clergy, or a psychotherapist.

All too often, people make mistakes they can't take back. Unless you or your kids are being abused or face immediate danger, there is usually time to think about an intelligent response to most problems.

Illusion Four

No matter what I do, he's always overreacting.

While this may be true (some people simply overreact to life) it's also symptomatic of some very typical passive-aggressive interactions, especially between two people embroiled in a divorce. For example, are you conveniently forgetting to inform your ex about your child's parent-teacher conference so it's already too late when you tell him and he won't be able to come? And to top that off, you tell your kid that Daddy wasn't really interested in attending?

That kind of behavior, when one party manipulates the other by undermining shared commitments, in this case "forgetting" to provide critical information that can be helpful, can be very provocative, triggering a totally unnecessary reaction from the aggrieved parent.

Does that sound familiar?

Another Day, Another Jam

War and Peace: Don't Let Your Ex Trigger You

Consider the woman who finds herself triggered by her husband's pretty colleague. She thinks, "Oh my God, he's going to leave me for that girl. She's gorgeous, and I'm not." In response to the trigger, she becomes needy and demanding, which outrages her spouse.

What's going on here? Why is she so upset?

Triggers activate complexes, which are both neurological and psychological. Complexes linger in our minds like undigested psychic experience from hurtful childhood moments. When triggered, they pop up to the surface and take over, making us behave irrationally.

If she digs deeper, she might recall being affected by an absentee father and by a mother who dated around for years. This woman hasn't seen a lot of men stick around, and she hasn't come to terms with the pain she felt whenever a new man exited her life. She is insecure when it comes to commitment. That's her complex, and it goes back to her childhood.

You gain control of your complexes by unveiling what triggers you, and why. In this way, you begin to objectify your experience—something only human beings can do.

Identifying your trigger and acknowledging that your response is out of line is one good step toward objectification, but it won't get you all the way there. People will tell you that knowing what they're doing wrong simply isn't enough to stop them from doing it. Even if she recognizes that her jealousy goes back to her experience as a kid, the woman in the example above will still feel jealous. Complexes won't just go away because you've had an "aha" moment; you need to integrate them into your adult life so they begin to lose their toxicity.

Change may be slow, but it's exactly how it happens when there are substantial things to change, whether it's with a professional or through your own solitary efforts. So, the same words and behaviors will still trigger your complexes, but because you are now more conscious of them—because you have objectified them as entities in and of themselves—you will start feeling more in control.

Trigger and Response

With your ex-spouse in mind, think of four comments or actions that have stung you in the past few weeks and triggered a response. Perhaps that response reminds you of something that may have happened when you were young.

This is the work of using the present moment to understand the past.

1. Comment/action:

My response:_____

Reminds me of: _____

2. Comment/action:

My response:_____

Reminds me of: _____

3. Comment/action:

My response: _____

Reminds me of: _____

4. Comment/action:

My response:_____

Reminds me of: _____

5. Comment/action:

My response:_____

Reminds me of: _____

The Repetition Compulsion in Action

Now that you've identified some of your triggers, consider your response to each of them. When activated, childhood complexes can get us to behave in ways that resemble one or more of the character traps we just described. For example, if a trigger causes you to feel vulnerable, you may fall temporarily into the victim role. But that same trigger might cause another person with a different history to feel angry, and bring out the avenger. The way you handled the original injury typically determines the character of your reaction, so let's look at the three ways children tend to adapt to their experiences, because after all, many of our adult responses to crisis originate in our childhood.

The Accepting Child

Some children accept their experience of abuse, neglect, or other hurt as normal. When these kids become adults, they are blind to the maladaptive nature of this treatment. In their marriage or divorce, they don't see that certain actions are wrong because they don't know better.

EXAMPLE
What's a Few Drinks?

Chelsea couldn't see Teddy's drinking problem. He would come home late, claiming that he was at work, and it took years for her to realize that Teddy was really working on his Jack Daniels at the bar. He wasn't abusive to Chelsea, but he was neglectful, and he floated from job to job.

Chelsea: "What are you doing?"

Teddy: "It's just a little drinking, I'll get over it."

Chelsea: "You can't do this; we need the money."

Teddy: "You don't understand me!"

Chelsea: "I understand, sweetheart. Just drink less, please. It's better for all of us."

Two months later

Teddy rolls in late again, having lost yet another job. The problem here is that Chelsea's dad also had two to three cocktails every night. His habits were woven into her childhood.

"From the Couch"

Chelsea is in denial of Teddy's drinking problem. It's obvious to us, and it's obvious to her, but her childhood experience makes it normative. As a little girl, Chelsea didn't want to believe her dad was impaired, so she convinced herself that this was the way families operated.

A person who didn't grow up in this environment would have dealt more harshly with Teddy early on. This would have been better for him—he may have even sought treatment. Alternatively, the marriage could have fallen apart, which would probably have been in everyone's interest. Teddy's drinking is dangerous and is simply unacceptable.

Did You Know?

If you're a Chelsea, and there are many of you out there, you are what Alcoholics Anonymous calls an "enabler." Many alcoholics are married to spouses who look the other way and thereby encourage their behavior. Check out Al-Anon, a non-profit support group devoted to the family members of alcoholics. Drinking is a problem that won't just go away. It requires intervention, and keep in mind, it's loving to help someone you care about get better.

The Child Who Identifies with the Victim

Instead of denying their hurts, some children identify with the victim, whether the victim be their mother, their father, or the child him or herself. As adults, these individuals seek relationships where their painful memories can be re-created in the hope of "righting" a past "wrong." While you're never responsible for another person's abuse, you can provoke the very thing you dread.

EXAMPLE

New Guy at the Office

Bernie was raised with five siblings. As if getting attention wasn't hard enough in this busy household, his mother adored his bratty but brilliant younger brother. Bernie always felt second best.

While Bernie has done well in life and holds a stable job, his self-esteem is fragile. This is Bernie's trigger point. He can easily feel like the odd man out when he senses competition for the attention of people he cares about.

One day, Alice, his wife of five years, returns from a business meeting talking about the new associate, Patrone.

Alice: "He is so smart. He makes my life a lot easier."

Bernie: "Really?"

Alice: "Yeah. He knows what he's doing. I appreciate him."

Bernie: "I don't usually hear you talk this way about people."

Alice: "What do you mean?"

Bernie: "How can you come into my house talking about another man? Who do you think you are?"

Alice: "Bernie, you're starting again!"

Bernie (getting up from his chair in a threatening way): "I don't want you talking to this guy. I'm not sure I want you working there anymore."

Alice: "What?"
Bernie: "You heard me!"
Alice (stammering): I don't understand."

Three months later

Alice is browsing in the bookstore and finds herself wandering into a section full of divorce books. She selects one and can't put it down.
"What am I going to do?" she starts thinking.

"From the Couch"

It doesn't take a psychiatrist to understand Bernie's trigger point. His self-esteem is like Swiss cheese. As a child, Bernie felt displaced by a smart, younger brother, leaving him feeling like a victim, and he continues to identify with that role. He now subtly recreates this sense of abandonment with Alice, who simply met a new colleague at work. Bernie's trigger is jealousy over her new acquaintance, and his response is paranoia and anger.

This isn't the first time Alice has dealt with Bernie's jealousy. He is constantly criticizing her, and he is always concerned with where she is, what she is doing, and who she is with. He eggs her on to reject him, which only fuels his concern over being second best; and it's getting old and suffocating for Alice. She's considering divorce more every day. If Bernie wants to stay in this relationship, he will need to know his trigger point, understand how he overreacts, and consciously decide to change.

The Child Who Identifies with the Bully

Other children identify with the aggressor. If their father beat them or their mother yelled at them, they may do the same to others. The psychology here is, "if you can't beat 'em, join 'em."

EXAMPLE
The Best Defense Isn't Always a Good Offense

Nikki had a tough childhood. Her parents loved her, but they divorced when she was young, leaving her with a lot of free, unsupervised time. The kids in the neighborhood had more chances to bully her—and they did.

Over time, Nikki learned that the best defense is a good offense. One day, at the age of 10, two tough 12-year-olds tried to beat her up, saying "you're ugly, you have no money, and you dress like trash."

After months of abuse and fear, she made a plan to protect herself. She surprised one of her bullies with a kick to the crotch and punched the other in the nose. Nobody messed with her after that.

Fast forward 30 years

Nikki's ex-husband, Liam, is constantly critiquing her parenting of their 16-year-old daughter, Sharon.

Liam: "I don't like that boy Sharon is dating."

Nikki: "He doesn't look so bad to me."

Liam: "He's just up to no good, I don't trust your judgment."

Nikki "You don't what?"

Liam: "She's 16, Nikki. She shouldn't be hanging out with this guy!"

Nikki (beginning to lose control): "I don't care what you think, my daughter will date who she wants, you condescending jerk!"

Liam: "What did I say?!"

Nikki (getting up to leave the room): "I'm not talking to you."

Liam: "You're crazy. Don't do this, we're talking about our child."

Nikki is out the door. They don't communicate for a week.

"From the Couch"

Nikki is triggered by Liam's criticism. It's true that criticism doesn't go over well in any divorce (or marriage, for that matter), but she finds it especially hurtful. She experiences his comment as a direct threat to her self-esteem, and it harkens back to memories of being ridiculed as a kid. Like Bernie, her self-esteem is full of holes. In this case, however, her response is to punish her opponent.

People sometimes complain about being "hurt" or "abused" and have little insight beyond their outrage. As psychiatrists and psychologists, we dig deeper, asking ourselves *why* these individuals react as they do. In this case, we see that Nikki adapted to her childhood pain by identifying with the aggressor. To the detriment of her family, she carries this posture into her adult relationships.

Nikki and Bernie present good examples of the compulsion to repeat our past. Bernie recreates the rejection he experienced as a kid, reinforcing his belief that he isn't valuable. Nikki can't see that her childhood trauma prevents her from constructively accepting criticism. Sadly, she encourages the disrespect she so desperately tries to combat. As a result, Liam won't take her seriously, and Sharon is probably smiling quietly in the corner, knowing that she can get away with whatever she wants.

Which Child Is Inside of You?

We can't possibly know the inner workings of every child, but anecdotal evidence shows that those who tend to be more timid probably fall into the similar roles of the accepting child or the victim. Those who are more aggressive tend to become the bully. Everyone's dynamic is different, and the way you respond to a trigger isn't solely based on your upbringing; it has to do with who you are at your core and how you have learned to adapt to the wounds of childhood. In the end, it's all about how you adjust to your current situation without letting your previous history dictate your current actions.

Writing Your Own Story

Patients come to me because they want their pain to end, but they don't always want to change. The great task of a therapist is to help people make changes they'd rather not make. We all get comfortable in our emotional states; we use these narratives to help define who we are. For example, it's easy to get stuck believing that life won't cut you a break and that the world is hopelessly unfair. Sounds like a victim who rarely sees her own actions objectively.

Psychiatrists aren't moral judges, and it's often impossible to determine who is more to blame when a couple breaks up. We help patients with their personal psychology so they can free themselves of past burdens and live happier lives going forward.

No one is keeping score! Except maybe you and your ex.

When I see a new patient, I may ask her to think of me as an editor. I invite her to step out of the protagonist's role and into the author's chair. Once you take charge of your own story you can increase your chances of actually living it.

My Story—My Life—Right Now

The questions that follow are designed to help you become the author of your own situation, which you can answer by yourself or with the help of a therapist. When you feel the impulse to write down your answers, make sure you do it!

Recording your thoughts will create an emotional inventory and putting your struggles and achievements into words can only help. It will also aid in tracking your development. Marking progress is a key step on the road to succeeding with your divorce.

Grief:

Am I grieving?

What stage am I in today?

Regression:

In what ways am I regressing?

How easily do I bounce back when I temporarily regress?

Do I believe some of the illusions that get people into trouble?

Character Traps:

Am I exhibiting evidence of a character trap?

Which one, and to what extent?

Is my ex exhibiting evidence of a character trap?

Which one, and to what extent?

Triggers:

Does my ex trigger me? What are my reactions?

Do my children trigger me? What are my reactions?

Can I objectify the triggers and render them less powerful?

Complexes:

When I am triggered, does it bring up old hurts from childhood?

What memories from earlier years may be contributing to my vulnerability?

Am I blaming my ex for any unresolved issues from my childhood?

Healing:

Am I healing from this divorce?

Am I moving toward acceptance, or are my emotions so powerful, that I can't move on?

What can I possibly do to change this? Would talking to someone help?

Pragmatic Advice:

How can I take better care of myself?

What legal help do I need?

Do I have enough financial insight?

Am I ensuring that I'm safe and respected?

Spirituality:

Has my spiritual life suffered during my divorce?

Do I reach out to people in the community or am I withdrawing from others?

How important (or not important) is my spiritual life. How can I turn this around?

My Children:

Are my kids developing properly?

In what way do they grieve the divorce?

How are they managing in school?

Am I depending on them too much?

Am I keeping them out of the divorce as much as possible?

Do they need to talk to someone?

What legal protection (if any) do they require?

Past, Present, and Future

The great American playwright Eugene O'Neill tells us in *Long Day's Journey into Night*, "The past is the present, isn't it? It's the future, too."

According to Harville Hendrix, author of *Getting the Love You Want: A Guide for Couples* (1988), we marry for two reasons. The first is that we believe we have found someone who can love us like no one else—our soul mate. The second is we marry someone who can unconsciously trigger our negative complexes. We pick the woman who will withhold love in the same way our mother did, or we choose the husband who is as cold as our father was. This, as we have said is the *repetition compulsion*—the theory that we're compelled to relive childhood injuries in adult life.

Well, this needn't be the case for you. People can change, and the future can be better. You can prevent yourself from repeating the past by knowing your internal complexes and healing them. Hopefully, we have given you the tools in this book to investigate them. We do have free will, after all. You're not stuck with what you're given. You don't have to stay in an unhappy relationship. You can learn from your childhood, unveil the meaning behind your triggers, and make changes.

With that in mind, it's important to know about your complexes because you don't want childhood memories taking charge of your adult life and causing you to act irrationally. You don't want to act violently toward your ex. You don't want to share intimate details with your kids that aren't necessary. You don't want to escalate a pointless legal battle.

You want to be an adult, in control, so that you can move on with your divorce. You have that choice, and on top of that, you have the responsibility to make things right for your children.

SCRAPBOOK
WHAT I'VE LEARNED ABOUT MY EX

I know he loves his kids and is a good father, but I was surprised by how his need to have a girlfriend right away really took priority over his own children.

I am learning how hard it is to truly accept another person who is wired differently than me and who operates from a different worldview. Though I do intellectually, I have a hard time accepting them emotionally, and that inability drives me nuts.

I naively thought that he would be accepting when I told him I could no longer work through our issues in therapy and that I wanted a divorce while our son was still very young. I couldn't imagine that he was happy or satisfied in the same marriage that made me so miserable. I was wrong. As I experienced my ex's rage (expressed in mostly passive-aggressive ways), I felt unfathomable guilt and anger toward him for making things so difficult. I have had to learn how to keep his anger from paralyzing or annihilating me. I have come to realize that I was naive to think that ending our marriage would be a relief for him. I learned that my ex had a right to all of his feelings even if they were difficult for me to deal with.

Resentment knows no boundaries.

I wanted her to be all right, but I wanted her to be all right without me.

Notes

This space is for you—to remember what's important, to doodle, to make plans ...

CHAPTER 5

The Biology of
Anger and Anxiety

When Your Mind Misbehaves

Depending on your temperament, chemistry, and past experience, different parts of your brain become stimulated by stressful circumstances. With divorce, you may develop an increased feeling of vulnerability, which can undermine your ability to be patient and maintain the reasonable behavior you need in order to manage this tough period in your life. Sometimes, the brain simply spins out of control.

In the preceding chapters, we presented a feeling-based approach to understanding your personality and the sources of your distress. Now we're going to look at *red braining* (disabling anger) and *mind loops* (disabling anxiety), two particularly difficult responses to triggers. Some people are biologically and experientially prone to red braining while others are more likely to respond to stress by mind looping. And, some have to endure both.

Red braining is difficult because it's so public; your ex or your children can be damaged by your behavior if you lose control. When your anger is triggered by fatigue, disappointment, or fear, all hell may break loose and nobody wins.

Triggers that precipitate mind loops are either internal or external, and the resulting anxiety tends to be privately experienced. Because it's so personal, few people know how much you're suffering. Red braining, on the other hand, is highly situational, and the way you handle the trigger that precipitates your anger can make it better or worse.

Solutions for red braining and mind loops are similar. They involve managing your triggers so that you don't overreact. You've already explored the origins of your complexes and what pushes your buttons; now we'll discuss how to handle that moment when you're about to lose control. Aside from objectification, pragmatic techniques developed over the last 20 years have been useful to patients in my practice. They are rooted in mental, physical, and spiritual approaches to your emotional life.

According to a 2009 study by the National Institute of Mental Health, more than 25 percent of adult Americans qualify for a psychiatric diagnosis each year. Since divorced and separated adults report almost twice as much psychological distress than the married population (Schoenborn, 2004), one can only imagine how much anger and anxiety is out there. We hope the practical methods you'll find in this chapter will help put you back in the driver's seat, without resorting to medication.

Your Red Brain and Gray Brain: How They Work

Everyone understands what it's like to lose control. When you're triggered, you can almost watch as your "Red Brain" takes over and you say or do things that you regret soon after. We all do it, whether married, single, or divorced. These outbursts can be directed at our spouses or our children. It should come as no surprise that power struggles and regression often provoke increased Red Brain behavior.

The "Gray Brain," on the other hand, is our voice of reason. It enables us to act rationally in the face of daunting circumstances. The Gray Brain is a colloquialism for the thinking and inhibitory functions of the frontal lobe and prefrontal cortex of the brain.

I developed the terms Red and Gray Brain in tandem with Phyllis Straus, an exceptional psychologist working in Israel. We created a course to help those involved in high-conflict marriages and found the terms remarkably useful when working with couples. They understood intuitively that there was a reactive switch that could be triggered by their kids or their partner. The experience of not feeling loved and respected or perceiving insults to one's ideas or positions were particularly jarring to our participants, as they probably are to you, as well.

When threatened, the Red Brain undermines the Gray Brain, commandeering our mental energy to protect the self. Scientifically, our mind handles dangerous situations by shutting down normal thinking in favor of a "fight or flight" mentality. In the wild, our ancestors responded quickly to threats by escaping or attacking. In marriage and divorce, the threat is rarely life and death, but the brain often reverts to survival mode because of the power of stress and regression. It feels easier to simply run away or instinctively attack the problem.

Rage Attacks: Taking Charge of Anger

Red Brain arousal is emotionally stressful and physically painful in some cases, and it generally increases the likelihood of accidental injury. Chronic agitation can contribute to dysfunction in many spheres of life, leading to physical distress or mental illness. It can also foster addictive coping methods, like drug or alcohol consumption, or overeating.

Your "Red Braining" will also affect your kids, who need a stable emotional environment. Your children need to focus on normal development and not on surviving a set of angry and unpredictable parents. When a child doesn't know when one

131

of his parents may fly off the handle, either at each other or at him, it can make the youngster's life worrisome and unsafe.

Marriage, divorce, and parenting all require a high level of Gray Brain activity—seeing things clearly and honestly, negotiating, compromising, and acting with patience, not to mention with respect. Emotionally smart people recognize the threats that trigger their Red Brain and deal with them by doing their best to use their Gray Brain. Understanding the source of your feelings, recognizing your cognitive distortions, changing your biological state, and infusing yourself with acceptance and spirituality can benefit individuals suffering the effects of Red Braining.

You've examined your triggers and explored the ways in which you respond. Is your Emergency Response System ready to handle whatever incoming fire might be heading your way?

WHAT PUSHES YOUR BUTTONS?

- Your ex swears at you (again), calling you a bleeping bleep!
- Your ex-wife accuses you (again) of ruining everything.
- Your ex calls you "useless" and a "loser."
- Your ex is deliberately late with Child Support payments.
- Your ex thinks you're a bad parent and complains about you to your friends and your kids.
- Your ex bombards you with demands by text and email.
- Your ex makes plans with your kids without consulting you.
- Your ex hangs up on you whenever he or she feels like it.

Ten Solutions for Red Brain Anger

1. **Be aware of how you feel before you spin out of control.**
   Part of gaining control over your emotions and your actions is by understanding how you respond to different situations, words, and behaviors. If you know a certain trigger makes you crazy angry, you may be able to prevent yourself from making a bad mistake.

> *"I count him braver who overcomes his desires than him who conquers his enemies; the hardest victory is the victory over self."*
> Aristotle

2. **Slow down! Remember good boundaries. Keep it safe!**
   Boundaries are essential. If you don't protect yourself, then you can't take care of anyone else in your life, especially your children. For your sake, and for theirs, know your limits. Be savvy. Don't assume that your ex has your best interests at heart. And, if you ever feel like you or your kids are in danger, don't hesitate. Get help.

> *"Good fences make good neighbors."*
> Robert Frost

3. **Walk away from the situation if you—or your ex-spouse—lose control.**

Walking away from a heated argument is the best way to prevent it from escalating. Your goal isn't to win every battle between you and your ex; it's to make things right for your kids. Walking away, hanging up the phone, or choosing not to respond to a hostile email, provides each of you the chance to cool down so that you don't say or do something you may regret later.

> *"When things go wrong, don't go with them."*
> Anonymous

4. **When you're upset by something that you hear, ask if he or she *really* meant it or simply spoke impulsively out of anger.**

We say things we don't mean all the time. I do it, you do it, and your ex is no exception to the rule. Questioning whether what was said was really intended gives your ex the opportunity to think it over. She may decide that the comment was too harsh or untrue; he may even take it back. This active listening technique also gives you the opportunity to think before you react. You may be able to avoid fights this way.

> *"Supreme excellence consists in breaking the enemy's resistance without fighting."*
> Sun Tzu

5. **Work off agitated energy through exercise, which can help reduce the rawness of your feelings and can change the biochemistry of your brain.**

   The human body is powerful, and with our desk jobs and automobiles most of us don't use it to its full potential. Physical activity affects the way we think by altering our levels of hormones and neurotransmitters. After people exercise, they tend to feel better.

   > *"Exercise is really important to me—it's therapeutic. So if I'm ever feeling tense or stressed or like I'm about to have a meltdown, I'll put on my iPod and head to the gym or out on a bike ride along Lake Michigan with the girls."*
   > Michelle Obama

6. **Discover the grandeur of nature. Nature is a healer.**

   Nature isn't only for the anxious; it's for everyone. We sometimes get so caught up in the drama of our lives that we forget that there is a world out there bigger than us. When you're angry or upset, take a walk outside. Notice the sounds and smells of your environment and consider the beauty of nature. It may just calm you down.

   > *"Let us spend one day as deliberately as Nature, and not be thrown off the track by every nutshell and mosquito's wing that falls on the rails."*
   > Henry David Thoreau

7. **Prepare yourself (and your ex-spouse) for difficult discussions. Good preparation will engage the Gray Brain and facilitate more constructive results.**
Some conversations between you and your ex will naturally raise more tensions than others. It's inevitable. The best way to get through these discussions is by preparing for them to the best of your ability. Think about your stance on a particular issue, and consider your ex's as well. Decide where you're willing to compromise and where you're not. Be prepared with good, logical arguments for what you want and coach yourself to be open to new ideas and approaches. You are the expert on how you and your ex interact, and if you're well prepared for tough discussions, they may just be more productive.

> *"Our minds can shape the way a thing will be because we act according to our expectations."*
> Federico Fellini

8. **Have a Plan B if things heat up too much. For instance, know when to call in a third party when required (therapist, lawyer, clergy, or other authorities). You may want to consult a psychotherapist in order to design the healthiest way to use outside assistance when the situation calls for it.**
There may be subjects that you and your ex-spouse simply cannot discuss on your own, and that's okay. A good solution is to seek third-party assistance. For example, you and

your ex may Red Brain at each other every time you meet to discuss the custody arrangement. In this case, there is nothing wrong with holding off on these conversations until you are in the presence of your respective attorneys. When it comes to your safety, backup plans are crucial. When people Red Brain, they do and say stupid things. If you ever feel like you're in danger, call the appropriate authorities. If you're the one who gets out of control, get help for yourself.

> *"You don't live in a world all your own.*
> *Your brothers are here, too."*
> Albert Schweitzer

9. **Psychotherapy and cognitive behavioral techniques are very helpful. Learn your own trigger points and how to reduce your own Red Braining.**
   This book is all about self-awareness and how empowering it can be. Psychotherapy isn't only for people with serious mental problems. It's for those who want to improve themselves or learn how to better handle tough times. If you're having trouble with some of the things we discussed in this book, consider the assistance of a professional.

> *"Most powerful is he who has*
> *himself in his own power."*
> Marcus Annaeus Seneca

10. **Psychopharmacology is sometimes useful on a temporary basis.**

Medication has helped millions of people. It isn't effective or recommended for everyone, but there are times when it can be useful. Talk to your doctor and do your own research. Weigh the advantages against the disadvantages of side effects and cost. Medication won't solve all of your problems, but it may make it easier to cope if you're having trouble doing so on your own.

> *"Suffering isn't ennobling; recovery is."*
> Christian N. Bernard

Ten Solutions for Red Brain Anger
(The Refrigerator Magnet Version)

1. Be aware of how you feel before you go out of control.
2. Slow down! Remember good boundaries. Keep it safe!
3. Walk away from the situation if you—or your ex-spouse—lose control.
4. When you're upset by something that you hear, ask if he or she *really* meant it or simply spoke impulsively out of anger.
5. Work off agitated energy through exercise, which can help reduce the rawness of your feelings and can change the biochemistry of your brain.
6. Discover the grandeur of nature. Nature is a healer.
7. Prepare yourself (and your ex-spouse) for difficult discussions. Preparing properly will engage the Gray Brain and facilitate more constructive results.
8. Have a Plan B if things heat up too much. For instance, know when to call in a third party when required (therapist, lawyer, clergy, or other authorities). You may want to consult a psychotherapist in order to design the healthiest way to use outside assistance when the situation calls for it.
9. Psychotherapy and cognitive behavioral techniques are very helpful. Learn your own trigger points and how to reduce your own Red Braining.
10. Psychopharmacology is sometimes useful on a temporary basis.

Mind Loops: Taking Charge of Anxiety

A *mind loop* occurs when a person regresses and the mind attempts to control the uncontrollable by looping furiously through emotional cycles, which causes more anxiety. It's like a series of short theatrical scenes, repeating themselves over and over until they commandeer your psyche.

Everybody knows what it's like to go to sleep at night and to be kept awake by intrusive words, images, or ideas. Anxious thoughts generate anxiety, which generate more anxious thoughts.

The mind loop concept is borrowed from the field of neurolinguistic programming. In psychiatry, this phenomenon is also called *obsessive thinking*. The mind loop aptly describes the actual experience of this process. Here is a typical example.

Will I Ever Be Okay?

Will I be okay? ➙

I used to be so happy. I know
I can be happy again. ➙

But is anybody ever going to love me? ➙

I feel so lonely. ➙

Will I ever be okay?

This individual, let's call him Joe, is anxious about his divorce working out. He tries to offer himself some reassurance by reminding himself that he had been happy in the past. Here Joe probably starts to feel a bit better. But then his anxiety kicks back in with the question of whether he will ever be loved. This loops back to a feeling of despair, "I feel so lonely," and ultimately back to where he started, with "Will I ever be okay?"

There are hundreds of loops like this, and I have heard plenty in my office. Below, take a look at some common mind loops in divorce. Do any of these thought processes sound familiar?

Sue's Helplessness Loop

I feel helpless. ➙

I need him so much. ➙ *He doesn't care about me.* ➙ *But I have other people who care about me.* ➙ *But do they really?* ➙

What can I do? I am alone and desperate ➙

I feel helpless.

Sue recognizes how she feels. She even knows why she is feeling this way: she believes that she needs her ex, but she doesn't believe he cares. Sue tries to solve this problem by reminding herself that there are people who care about her, but she then dismisses the thought. She finally reveals a defeatist attitude: "What can I do? I am alone and desperate." This brings her back to feeling helpless.

With a bit of proactive planning, Sue can change. She can seek out friends and do her best to alter her outlook on the divorce; she doesn't have to end right back where she started.

Bill's Money Loop

I'm not made of money. ➙

She's gonna wipe me out. ➙ *Maybe we can work something out.* ➙ *All she cares about is herself.* ➙

I'm not made of money.

Bill is worried about his finances. He believes that his wife wants an excessive amount of money. He tries to reassure himself, but his mind loops back around, and he lands where he started, with nothing solved and his anxiety fueled.

When it comes to money, a lot of divorcing people get anxious. They don't know what to expect, or how they will fare once legal documents are signed. Bill hopes that they can "work something out," but he brings himself to the painful realization that "she doesn't really care about me." As with the previous mind loop, a proactive approach might break the cycle. Instead of fretting, Bill might come up with solutions, like talking to his accountant and his attorney about legal ways to protect his assets.

Colleen's Loyalty Loop

I'm so loyal. ➡

He betrayed me. ➡ *How can anyone do this to me?* ➡

He should pay for what he did to me. ➡

I'm so loyal.

Colleen begins with an affirmative statement about herself. Then she emphasizes the difference between her and her ex: she was loyal; he was not. We see confusion, frustration, and perhaps even anger enter into her third statement, "How can anyone do this to me?" This stems from a desire (which many of us have) for the world to be fair. But the world isn't fair, and Colleen doesn't want to accept this. She wants to make things "right" by "getting him back." She still thinks she deserves to take justice into her own hands because, once again, she is "so loyal."

This mind loop should remind you of the Avenger character trap. People often get stuck in a holier than thou mindset, believing that they have the right to do whatever is in their power to turn the tables on their ex. This is because "I was so good" and "he was so bad," as you see illustrated in Colleen's loop. The problem here is that people aren't meant to play God; we are given the privilege of living on this earth, and we should do so with integrity. It's unfortunate that life isn't always fair, but that's the way it is. Accepting this truth will get you and your kids farther than denying it ever will. It will help you move on.

Tom's Humiliation Loop

What are people thinking about me? →

Maybe I should go home. → *I can't stay in this church when they're all talking about me.* →
I don't want people talking about me! → *Look over there! They are talking about me. I know it.* →

What are people thinking about me?

Tom's first question reveals his anxiety over social acceptance. Before letting himself answer his own question, however, Tom decides that he should probably leave because "they're all talking about me." He has drawn a conclusion based on little to no evidence and without giving it much consideration. All Tom knows is that he doesn't want people talking about him. He tries to reassure himself that there is nothing to worry about, but the mind loop takes over and cycles back to his first thought, "What are people thinking about me?"

It's normal to wonder how others will react to your divorce. As we mentioned, the unfortunate reality is that not everyone will stick by your side. But not everyone will abandon you, either. Tom should consider that, with so much divorce in America, his is probably not the only one on people's minds. Besides, people in church have their own worries, which have nothing to do with him.

The flaw in this mind loop is present in its first component: "What are people thinking about me?" Inherent in this question is the ready-made judgment that people *are* thinking about him. But Tom has no proof of this. Biased questions often lead to biased answers.

This example exposes how mind loops take over. Tom can sit in church for hours, torturing himself with this loop playing over and over in his head. His attempts to think rationally are repeatedly thwarted by the powerful anxiety that motivates the mind loop.

Instead, he might ask himself, *"Am I mind looping?"* With this question, he would have a better shot at rebutting his thoughts, finding an effective solution, and thinking logically about the scenario.

Desiree's Health Loop

I'm sure I have cancer. →

But the doctor checked me out and said that I'm okay. → *But doctors make mistakes.* → *What's going to happen to my kids if I get sick?* → *There is no one to take care of me.* →

I'm sure I have cancer.

Desiree has been wondering for quite some time about the possibility of being sick. In fact, she's convinced herself that she has cancer. She presents sound evidence that she is healthy but her anxiety leads her to question the doctor. Desiree wonders about her kids' future and her own. With her anxiety mounting, her mind loops back to the original statement: "I'm sure I have cancer."

This mind loop is what happens when you refuse to believe the evidence that is right in front of you, opting instead for some bigger worry over things you can't control. Everyone getting divorced becomes anxious at some point—some more and some less—and Desiree's concern about who will care for her and her children is universal.

Some people under stress become preoccupied with their health. In fact, with this type of mind loop, the stress of divorce can cause people to worry excessively about everything and anything. If this kind of displacement happens to you, seek help, just as Desiree first did by visiting her doctor. You must accept the fact that sometimes you can't fix everything by yourself.

Pragmatic Ways to Handle Anxiety

Mind loops often appear at night, prior to falling asleep, and they may keep you awake. They may also emerge while you are driving, interfering with your concentration. Truthfully, they can take over at any time. It's as if the brain is convinced that if it just thinks hard enough about a problem it will be solved and the stress will disappear. It's like a glitch in the computer circuitry of the mind, and it simply doesn't work.

The more you obsess, the more you will continue obsessing. You can overcome mind loops, but you have to use a technique that works for you. In addition to gathering insight about the sources of your emotional state, we will present three other approaches to handling anxiety that have become increasing appreciated by psychiatrists and other mental health professionals. In simple terms, these are *thinking-based, brain/body-based,* and *spiritual-based treatment techniques.*

1. **Recognize the voice of your mind loops and how the same scripts keep hijacking you.**

   Awareness of a mind loop reduces its toxicity. If you watch as the script hijacks your thoughts, you can reduce it from high anxiety to mild annoyance. This is a thought-based technique that is used in cognitive-behavioral therapy, and it works on the assumption that, by altering the way you think about your mind loops, you can change your reactions.

2. **Remind yourself that this is just a mind loop. It will eventually go away.**

   Instead of saying, "Oh my God, I'm mind looping, what do I do?" try "Okay, I'm mind looping; it will come and go." You can tell yourself this because you know that mind loops are time limited and that the more you fight them, the longer they run. By changing the way you think about the loop, you change the way you respond.

Buddhists have a teaching called "nonattachment," and it can be applied here as well. The mind must detach itself from its own anxiety in order to heal. This can be achieved through awareness (objectification), practice, and, for some, meditation. People who are more mindful have an easier time letting go of negative, automatic thoughts (Frewen, Evans, Maraj, Dozois, and Partridge, 2008). Spiritual acceptance plays a role here, too. When you accept the loops you experience, it will be easier to do the work of letting them go.

3. **Choose to change your biological mind-set through physical activity.**
    A great way to remedy anxiety is by changing the chemical nature of your brain via physical action. This brain/body-based technique can be achieved by exercising, walking, dancing, showering, even taking a nice bath, all of which generate a neurotransmitter release, which calms you down.

    Research has demonstrated that laughter not only reduces stress, but also improves the functioning of your immune system (Bennett, Zeller, Rosenberg, and McCann, 2003), and studies repeatedly show that exercise reduces symptoms of anxiety, whether you are suffering from psychological or physical ailments (Herring, O'Conner, & Dishman, 2010).

4. **Seek the presence of a great friend and/or a beloved pet.**
    If you have a friend who can touch you in a comforting way—one that is neither sexual nor provocative—that

touch can be grounding. Having someone put an arm over your shoulder or touch your hand with understanding can reawaken the biological experience of connectedness, of not being alone. Just like running or laughing, this action can change the state of your mind.

When people receive social and emotional support, they report better mental and physical health, leading to greater life satisfaction. There is also less smoking, heavy drinking, physical inactivity, and obesity among those who receive social support (Strine, Chapman, Balluz, and Mokdad, 2008).

Reaching out, even when it's counterintuitive to do so because you don't believe that people will care, may introduce you to the very people who can bring you peace.

Lastly, we have our pets, because a sense of community is found not only among humans. Pets have a positive effect on blood pressure, cholesterol levels, and triglyceride levels, and they make you feel less alone (Centers for Disease Control and Prevention, 2007a).

5. **Experience the healing powers of nature.**
    Nature makes us aware of a world and purpose larger than ourselves. Whether it be cold, white snow, the sounds of summer by the seashore, or the smell of autumn leaves, we are small in the face of nature's grandeur.

    The emotional experience of connecting with nature can help put our anxieties into perspective. After all, what's loneliness in the face of the beautiful creations abundant in our world? In fact, a study of patients recovering from surgery found that those with plants or flowers in their hospital rooms experienced lower systolic blood pressure and reported lower anxiety, fatigue, and pain than did patients without plants or flowers in their room (Park and Mattson, 2009).

6. **If you're spiritually inclined, you may consider that "control is in God's hands and I give over my fears and trust to God."**
For many, faith can soothe like nothing else. Suffice it to say prayer or belief in God can calm the soul. What's a mind loop when you know that God is watching over you? Research shows that people who see God as loving report fewer symptoms of psychopathology than those who view God as distant (Bradshaw, Ellison, and Flannelly, 2008).

7. **Psychotherapy and cognitive-behavioral techniques may be appropriate.**
Traditional, insight-oriented psychotherapy gives you tools to deal with mind loops by awakening you to the complexes that lie behind them. You understand that you're not only upset with an ex-spouse who hurt you, but with something that happened in your youth. You come to realize that you're no longer a child and that you're more competent than you think.

Cognitive-behavioral therapy (CBT) provides you with specific techniques to help you place mind loops in context. CBT teaches you how your mind thinks and how it maximizes anxiety. It is a proven treatment for anxiety disorders (Stewart and Chambless, 2009).

8. **Sometimes psychopharmacology is useful on a temporary basis.**

   If mind loops are becoming chronic and life depleting, medication may be useful on a temporary basis. Find out what works so that you can step up and focus on what your children really need from you. Anti-anxiety agents, antidepressants, and other prescriptive medicines are available if required. You can find more information in the back of this book.

The Intelligent Consumer: A Primer on Treatment

We have introduced four different approaches to mental health: feeling-based, thought-based, brain/body-based, and spirituality-based. Now let's review what each one is about and who can provide the help that you may need.

Insight-oriented psychotherapy is a feeling-based approach to mental health. Whether its psychoanalysis, supportive psychotherapy, existential analysis, or imago therapy, it all comes down to the therapist helping you understand your feelings so you can get in touch with their source, objectify their experience, and master them.

In the last chapter, we introduced you to a feeling-based approach. We reviewed how triggers raise powerful feelings, and how those feelings are connected to memories, which form complexes. The more a patient understands this chain of events, going backward and forward, the better able he or she is to objectify, detoxify, and integrate the experience into a mature mindset.

For comprehensive information on Freudian psychoanalysis, contemporary analysis, existential therapy, and other contemporary therapeutics, you might want to take a look at the *Textbook of Psychotherapeutic Treatments* (2009) by Glen O. Gabbard, M.D.

A thought-based approach to a psychological problem, whether it be depression, anxiety, or personality disorders, has its origins in the work of Aaron Beck, M.D. in the 1960s. If you're interested in his work, you can check out some of his books, such as *Cognitive Therapy and Emotional Disorders* (1976), or more recently, *Scientific Foundations of Cognitive Theory and Therapy of Depression* (Clark, Beck, and Alford, 1999). Cognitive-behavioral therapy theorizes that feelings are a product of mistaken thinking. If a person, therefore, corrects his mistaken belief, the feeling—whether it is depression or anxiety—will abate. CBT therapists give homework and offer pragmatic labels for the ways in which your thinking has gone wrong.

Contemporary CBT therapists often integrate spiritual approaches to healing, such as mindfulness, which research has shown to be effective.

The third approach presented here is brain/body-based, and it assumes that both the brain and body are influencing the mind. It encourages you to treat yourself well, by exercising, eating healthily, and sleeping properly. When the situation calls for it, the brain/body approach also uses medicine as a tool for biological change.[1]

If you don't get enough sleep or have proper nutrition your brain will interfere with the clear functioning of your mind. Physical damage to your brain—like a concussion—will do the same thing. You can optimize your brain's functionality and thereby maximize your mind's ability, in a number of ways. Omega-3 fatty acids have been shown to increase mood and clarify thought, while vigorous, regular exercise has been documented time and again to increase vitality, decrease anxiety, and promote a sense of general well-being.

As a psychiatrist, I'm comfortable prescribing pharmaceuticals, but in most cases, I see them as temporary in nature. Whether I use an antidepressant, an anti-anxiety agent, or an antipsychotic medicine, I rarely have people on medication for indeterminate periods of time. That said, there are those who benefit from long-term use. We discover whether this is the case by weaning a patient off of her medication and seeing how she does. If the disturbing pattern of thought or behavior returns, we can determine that it's in the patient's best interest to remain on a long-term dose.

Finally, there is the spirituality-based approach to health. Many psychotherapists are now savvy to the healing powers of prayer and mindfulness, and they incorporate them into treatment. It's now common for therapists to teach mindfulness or inquire about the nature of a patient's prayer life.

While research shows these practices to be helpful in and of themselves, as with mind/body-based approaches, spiritual practices often do not provide sufficient treatment. They are,

---

[1] For more information on pharmaceuticals, refer to the Appendix on Psychiatric Medicine.

however, invaluable as complementary methods to healing psychological wounds.

Now that you're aware of the different types of treatment available to you, let's review the kinds of professionals who can provide you with help. Choosing a therapist isn't an easy task.

You want to find someone that you can trust and has the tools to help you. On your first visit, you may not know whether the counselor you see is right for you, but keep in mind that not every therapist works for every person—it's okay to be picky.

Finding a Therapist Who is Right for You

Psychiatrists: Psychiatrists are medical doctors who have advanced training in both brain biology and human psychology. They provide comprehensive care that includes psychiatric evaluations (involving the psychological and biological functioning of patients), writing for medical tests that may be required, and providing treatment, which includes psychotherapy and medication, when required.

Psychologists: Psychologists are professionals who have typically received their Ph.D. or a master's degree in psychology. They are trained to assess psychological states and to provide a variety of psychotherapeutic treatments. Some perform psychological testing, which is a verified, valid way of objectifying a patient's problems, and there are those who practice in a particular area of interest, whether in an educational or therapeutic setting.

Social Workers: Social workers have typically received their master's degree in social work. Their background is in social systems as well as in individual psychology. Most social workers are great at providing therapy and at integrating care into the larger social network. They sometimes work in private offices, but just as often work in clinics and in schools.

Clinical Nurse Specialists: This advanced degree is the equivalent of a Ph.D. in nursing. The clinical nurse specialist who specializes in psychiatry can act very much like a psychiatrist. He or she can interview a patient, write for medical tests, provide therapy, and even prescribe medication.

Pastoral Counselors: Clergy who bear this distinction have taken extra training to certify them to provide psychotherapy. They couple their spiritual expertise with an interest in human psychology. The pastoral counselor is not the average priest or rabbi who will triage you to someone else when they've reached the limit of what they can provide—this is truly a psychological professional who also happens to be a member of the clergy.

Drug Counselors: Drug counselors hail from a variety of backgrounds and, depending on the state, require different levels of training. You should make certain, however, that the person you're working with has been certified in drug and alcohol treatment. Drug counselors are prepared to encourage and foster healthy behavior in addicts, and to help both them and their families cope. You'll find them working with groups as well as in one-on-one settings.

Notes

This space is for you—to remember what's important, to doodle, to make plans ...

CHAPTER 6

Nutrition, Exercise, and Sleep

When Food and Fitness Are
Your Greatest Friends

For the average American family, which is not as healthy as it should be, divorce presents an unwelcome health risk. The chances of your health improving naturally as a result of a divorce are slim to none. In fact, it's usually the opposite. Therefore, if you're getting divorced, you will need to pay extra attention to your nutrition, your fitness, and your general wellness, including your sleeping habits.

Let's start with food, because eating seems to be such a popular activity. What you eat is important because stress can compromise the immune system. One way to protect your body is to eat right and avoid environmental toxins. You have the rest of your life to look forward to, and we want you to enjoy it in good health.

How you eat is also critical. If you have a history of emotional eating, divorce will really test your self-control. Anxiety and despair can lead to over or under-eating, and disorders can form around your habits. If you choose to dine with a friend while discussing your ex, be alert to the range of emotions you experience. It's possible for a negative memory to become associated with a particular food, and that will only make things worse.

This chapter is all about helping you mitigate physical and emotional damage by forming healthy nutritional habits, embracing fitness, developing a general strategy for wellness, and learning good sleep habits. Now more than ever it's vital that you give yourself the love you deserve by treating your body well. Here are some helpful strategies and ways to begin.

A special thanks to Geri Brewster, RD MPH CDN, for helping us present an understandable approach to nutrition in divorce. Implementing these habits will benefit you and your children.

Whole Foods

Take a look at your shopping list. What type of food should you be eating? The benefits of "whole" foods have been well documented, especially vegetables, fruits, herbs, spices, nuts, and seeds. A whole food is not a food product. For example, that means you should be eating real fruit, not fruit candy, and real juice, not juice soda. When you're not able to eat "whole" foods try to eat "clean" foods that are minimally processed and preserved.

If you can, eat organically, too. Recent studies have linked numerous allergic reactions and other health issues with the pesticides and antibiotics that can be found in commercially processed foods. Do yourself and your kids a favor and eat as much organic or locally produced food as possible. Even if you can't always buy organic, there are certain foods on your family shopping list which should be purchased organic due to the high pesticide content in commercially produced foods. We'll list them for you here.

Recommended Fruits

Peaches Strawberries Apples Blueberries Nectarines Cherries Grapes Honeydew Avocado Pineapple Kiwi Mangos Cantaloupe Watermelon Grapefruit

Vegetables

Celery Bell peppers Spinach Kale Potatoes Onions
Sweet corn Sweet peas Asparagus Cabbage
Sweet potato Eggplant

Meats, Poultry, and Dairy

If at all possible, try to buy products that are organic. We eat what those animals ate, and if you've ever seen how cows and chickens are treated and fed, you know how bad it can be. What they consume alters the composition of the final product; it impacts the balance of fatty acids, nutrients, and toxic residues, which end up in your food. If you can't purchase certified organic meat, poultry, and dairy products, look for locally grown farmers who raise grass-fed beef and free-range chickens.

Fish

Avoid farmed fish. Try to eat the wild variety and those that aren't on the watch list because of toxicity. Presently, our recommendations include the following: Pacific cod, crab (Dungeness, stone, king, snow), Pacific halibut, spiny U.S. lobster, salmon (Alaska, Washington), albacore tuna (British Columbia), skipjack tuna, clams, Pacific cods and soles, flounders, sea scallops, shrimp (U.S., Canada), and squid.

For more information about your favorite seafood, check *www.seafoodwatch.org.* It is useful to check this site periodically as environmental conditions change.

Additionally, the Food and Drug Administration (FDA) and the Environmental Protection Agency (EPA) are advising women who may become pregnant, pregnant women, nursing mothers, and young children to avoid some types of fish, and to eat fish and shellfish that are lower in mercury.

Power Pack Your Pantry

The cornerstone of your diet should be nutrient-rich, brain-building, disease-fighting foods. Here are the basics for a pantry, fridge, and freezer that are clean and power-packed:

Vegetables

Alfalfa sprouts, Artichokes, Asparagus, Aubergene (Eggplant), Beans, Beets, Boy choy, Broccoli, Brussels sprouts, Cabbage, Carrots, Cauliflower, Celery, Chard, Chicory, Collards, Corn, Cucumber, Endive, Escarole, Garlic, Green or yellow beans, Jerusalem Artichoke, Jicama, Kale, Leek, Lettuce, Mung beans, Mushrooms, Okra, Onions, Parsnips, Peas, Peppers, Potatoes (white and red), Shallots, Spinach, Squash (green), Pumpkins, Radicchio, Radish, Rutabaga, Sea vegetables (seaweed, kelp), Squash, Sweet potato, Taro, Tomatoes, Turnips, Watercress, Water Chestnuts, Winter squash and Yams.

Fruits

Apples and Apple butter, Applesauce (unsweetened), Apricots, Avocado, Bananas, Berries (all types), Cherries, Kiwi, Lemon, Mango, Melon (all varieties), Nectarines, Papaya, Peaches, Pineapple, Plums, Prunes, Raisins and other Dried fruits (unsweetened).

Proteins

Meat: Chicken, Chicken broth, Turkey, Lamb and all Wild game.

Fish (fresh or canned): Cod, Halibut, Mackerel, Salmon, Tuna, and Trout.

Grains
Buckwheat, Kasha, Millet, Organic corn chips, Organic pancake mix, Rice (brown or wild), Quinoa and Whole grain breads.

Nuts, Seeds and Oils
Almonds and Almond oil, Cashews, Flaxseeds and Flaxseed oil, Hazelnuts, Olives and Olive oil, Pecans, Pumpkin oil and seeds, Sesame oil and seeds, Sunflower oil and seeds, Walnuts and Walnut oil, and Nut butters from nuts listed above.

Spices
Anise, Baking Powder, Baking Soda, Basil, Bay leaf, Cardamom, Celery Seed, Cinnamon, Coriander, Cumin, Dill, Dry Mustard, Egg Substitute, Fennel, Garlic, Ginger, Oregano, Parsley, Rosemary, Savoy, Tarragon, Thyme, Turmeric and Vinegar (all types except grain).

Detoxing
Nutritionists recommend many ways to detox, meaning to cleanse the body of the toxins that collect there after years and years of eating poorly. Some methods are more intense than others.

While going through the rigors of a divorce, a less intense, gentle cleansing diet is probably best. Once your divorce is behind you and you can take some time off to devote just to yourself, you can consider a more intense detox that can be done under the supervision of a healthcare practitioner. For now, we will begin the process of cleansing the harmful chemicals from your body and the toxic connections that certain foods may have had to your troubled marriage.

You can support your cleansing diet by eliminating many of the stored chemicals in your body by using various forms of detoxification including not only diet, but supplements, massage, and sauna.

Part of detoxing is supporting the body with the nutrients it needs to cleanse naturally, and that is why a clean, healthy diet is so important. Being conscious of what you ingest will help eliminate a variety of contaminants that make their way into your body.

Alkalinizing your body is a great way to facilitate the detoxification process. Foods that do this include vegetables, legumes, nuts, and seeds. Each are high in fiber, which also promotes another means of detox—regular bowel movements.

Your Three-Day Detox Menu

Breakfast: Upon waking, have a glass of filtered water with a squeeze of fresh lemon. Prepare your preferred herbal tea; if you are a coffee or caffeine consumer, prepare green tea. If you need a sweetener, use raw honey. Select from the following mixed fruit cup: berries, apples, pears, peaches or melons. Have a cereal or grain, for example, old-fashioned Irish oats, amaranth flakes, or quinoa flakes with one tablespoon of ground flax seeds, served with almond, rice or coconut milk. Add a protein source like raw almonds, cashews, or walnuts.

Mid morning: Have a green drink. You can prepare your own or purchase one already made or made fresh from your local health-food store juice bar.

Lunch: Choices may include a vegetable omelet with a side salad, a vegetarian bean based soup with a side salad, a salad of mixed greens topped with chickpeas, sprouts, and vegetables. Drink filtered water, which can be flavored with a splash of real (100 percent) unsweetened cranberry juice.

Mid-afternoon snacks: Fresh fruit and raw nuts or avocado and organic corn chips.

Dinner: Select a wild fish or organic poultry or meat. If you are a vegan, eat tofu or bean curd. Accompany with a variety of green vegetables such as broccoli, spinach, asparagus, kale, swiss chard, brussel sprouts, and non-green vegetables such as a squash blend (ratatouille), spaghetti squash, or roasted peppers. Serve alongside sweet potato, quinoa salad, or brown rice. Side salad with olive oil, apple cider vinegar, and herbs can accompany every evening meal.

After dinner: Poached pear, baked apple, or mixed berries, sprinkled with cinnamon.

Your Morning Routine

Now that you're cleansed, let's get you on the road to a healthy diet that you can maintain.

Let's begin with your morning routine. The first thing you should do is drink a glass of water. If you'd like, you can add a splash of unsweetened cranberry juice (the real thing—100 percent cranberry with no sweetener of any type). This juice is very tart so just a splash is all you'll need to help make your morning water that much more refreshing. A squeeze of lemon could work well, too. Drinking water is a good way to hydrate and cleanse your system while you're preparing either your tea or your coffee.

If you've never been a breakfast eater, this is probably a good time to start. Breakfast truly is the most important meal. Chances are that your day is going to be long and stressful, so the opportunity to get in a good meal will probably be a challenge.

You deserve a good breakfast. It will rehydrate and replete you after a night's sleep. It will provide you with protein and good fats to ensure that your blood sugar doesn't crash mid-morning. If you include a complex carbohydrate, it will provide you with needed fiber along with sustained energy.

Many of you are probably in the habit of grabbing a cup of coffee and a buttered roll or a bagel with cream cheese once you get to the office or after you drop the kids off at school. The burst of caffeine and the simple carbohydrates (if you've chosen a white flower roll or bagel) will provide an early-day energy surge, but a couple of hours later, they are sure to decrease your blood-sugar levels. What does this mean? You'll be noshing throughout the day, craving additional carbohydrates.

If you typically drink tea in the morning, it's a good idea to alternate with green tea. The literature suggests that, compared to black tea, green tea has additional antioxidant compounds that can benefit your health. If you are a coffee drinker, you may want to switch to half naturally decaffeinated. This way, you'll reduce your dependence on caffeine. Heaven knows, you'll be making plenty of adrenaline during your divorce, and we don't want you to be pushed too far into overdrive. Living constantly in a state of "fight or flight" can leave you drained and may lead to serious health consequences.

Studies show that reducing the simple carbohydrates in your diet and increasing your intake of fiber and protein can help you achieve and maintain a desirable body weight. This means cutting down on foods that are artificially high in sugar or made with white flour.

Breakfast

If you have time: Scrambled eggs and whole grain toast or slow cooked oats with chopped walnuts and cinnamon.

If you are packing to go: A hardboiled egg and whole grain toast or Greek yogurt (higher in protein) with granola or organic peanut butter or almond butter on whole grain toast.

If you are grabbing take out: Use your best judgment and make good choices!

Lunch
Here are three suggestions to get you started.

Menu #1
½ to 1 cup barley with non starchy vegetables,
4–5 ounces of broiled sole or flounder, seasoned with olive oil, garlic and herbs,
a green salad with ½ avocado and two tablespoons of walnut halves with flaxseed oil and lemon juice

Menu #2
4–5 ounces turkey breast sliced over ½–¾ cup brown rice with olive oil and two tablespoons chick peas
1 cup broccoli with 1 tablespoon of shredded almonds and 1 teaspoon olive oil, and 1 pear

Menu #3
¼ cup hummus on a mini whole wheat pita with black olives, lettuce and tomato,
with 10 ounces of vegetable soup

Dinner
It's best to complete your dinner at least three hours before retiring to bed. Generally, the later you eat, the lighter the food should be, with the least amount of simple carbohydrates and

single portions of complex carbohydrates, if any, as these get converted to and stored as fat. Nothing should be consumed after dinner, except herbal or decaf green tea or a non-caloric beverage or "food," such as sugar free or low sugar ice pops. This will not only help you keep your weight down and improve digestion; it will surely help you sleep better, too.

Menu #1
8–12 ounces chicken broth with ½ cup escarole
4–6 ounces of chicken breast
1 cup green and wax beans with 1 teaspoon olive oil
2 cups mixed greens salad with ½ avocado, 3 large olives, olive oil and red wine vinegar

Menu #2
4 ounces roast leg of lamb
1cup steamed cauliflower, with sweet onion and olive oil
mixed green salad with 2 tablespoons almond slivers and ⅓ cup Greek olives, tomatoes and tahini dressing

Menu #3
8 ounces roasted vegetable medley of squash, peppers, eggplant and asparagus over ⅔ cup quinoa, seasoned with olive oil and herbs and ½ cup three-bean salad

Snack Time!

These foods are good to eat throughout the day and before or after vigorous exercise:

1 tablespoon macadamia nut butter on a WASA Fiber Krisp
Water, seltzer, green tea

Organic blue corn chips with cheddar and salsa
4 ounces organic cottage cheese with berries
Hard boiled egg and organic soy chips

If you add any snacks of your own to this list, check carefully for their caloric and fat content as well as for "clean" ingredients. And since over-shopping usually leads to over-eating, short ingredient lists are always better.

Emotions and Food

Our bodies can usually handle quite a bit of stress, but living through a divorce can challenge anyone's constitution. As you know, we can keep up the good fight for only so long, before some part of us physically breaks down and our immune system becomes compromised. That could mean contracting a heavy cold, developing digestive problems, or something even worse, like a heart condition.

Donna's Story

When I was getting divorced I was miserable every night. I ate ice cream and guacamole to make the pain and loneliness disappear. After a few months, I had almost gained enough weight to become a second person who could keep myself company. One night, I went on a dating site and started filling out my personal profile. When they asked for body type, I was like, which one, happy me or sad me? I didn't know any longer which one I was or what I was becoming.

Donna, age 37

Each of us process stress differently, but we all face the reality of science. When tension and strife get to be too much, our body naturally tries to protect itself. Cortisol is a stress hormone responsible for increasing gastric-acid secretion and blood-sugar levels and suppressing the immune system. That can make you vulnerable to any number of ailments, and if your body releases too much cortisol it can interfere with your sleep pattern.

As your body pumps your bloodstream with hormones on a regular basis, it doesn't take into account any additional issues you may be going through, such as your divorce. For example, women may be trying to manage PMS and menopause during a divorce, while men may be trying to manage andropause, the male version of menopause. Your doctor should be able to assist you through these phases of life but ultimately it's up to you to figure out how to manage your own body.

Resistance to Eating Right

You probably know what happens when you get overly worried or mildly depressed from having too much on your mind. You either don't eat enough or you eat too much, especially too much of the wrong kinds of foods! Throughout the process of getting divorced, you may be at risk for doing either one.

It's probably time to step back and reassess your response to stress and your divorce. If you're not eating well—either too little or too much—are you simply regressing, falling back into the role of the obstinate child who pouts when she doesn't get her way? Except this time, you're an adult, and your pouting is unhealthy. Perhaps you're indulging your problems even further by falling into one of the character traps we discussed earlier. Victims are notorious for eating poorly, whether by eating too little, or indulging their hurts by eating too much.

Do you see yourself in one of these profiles? If so, the only one you're hurting by pretending otherwise is you. Actually, that's not true. You're probably also shortchanging a lot of others around you, most notably your children.

The human mind is very good at rationalizing self-defeating behavior that feels good in the moment. *"It doesn't matter" or "I will start a better diet tomorrow"* doesn't really cut it.

You are what you eat; there's no way around that, and you owe it to yourself and your kids to use all the helpful information at your disposal (and in this day and age there is plenty) to get your act together and get healthy!

This is also a good time for you to look into adding vitamins and supplements to your daily diet. Here are some suggestions for you to discuss with your doctor or healthcare provider to see what would be a good fit for you and your personal health condition.

To Supplement or Not

The Harvard University School of Public Health recommends that the average adult with no particular health issues should take a daily multivitamin with minerals as an insurance policy for continued good health. It also points out that it's important not to take too many vitamins.

Keep in mind, too, that men and postmenopausal women do not need to take a pill that includes iron. It's best to consult with your doctor and/or a certified nutritionist to determine what vitamins and supplements would be best for your particular needs. Be careful about going for the quick-fix approach, like buying things you see on TV and expecting them to change your life overnight. Be smarter than that. Healthy food, simple exercise, and mindfulness will always serve you well.

Your Kids and Food

Now that you're on your way to better eating, let's discuss feeding your children. With every new generation, things change. Hardly anyone learns food preparation in school anymore; home economics is a thing of the past. With both parents working and grandparents living far away, it's unlikely that someone is home preparing meals that you or your children get to observe.

Today, nearly everyone is raised on a steady stream of convenient, processed foods. While these meals can be ready in an instant, they are not always satisfying, let alone healthy. Often, people take care of dinnertime by eating out. But with the added expense that each spouse now takes on to maintain a separate household, some of that budget will need to be scaled back.

At the same time, because you may be seeing your kids less, mealtimes will probably become more valuable and you can do a lot to make them meaningful for everyone in your family.

First of all, slow down whenever possible. For example, if you see your kids only every other weekend, don't turn your meals into a fast-food frenzy.

Involve your kids in meal planning. You may want to join a CSA (Community Supported Agriculture) program and pick up fresh produce, meats, and eggs weekly, or attend a local farmers' market. Consider starting a garden in the spring, even if you just plant patio tomatoes or herbs. Mealtime is a great opportunity to bond with your kids. Preparing food, setting the table, and serving your inventions is all good parenting in action! When you make the most of it, everyone benefits.

Fitness

Simply eating better is a great first step toward improving your overall health. You are what you eat, and all that, but if you don't exercise, you significantly reduce your chances for a good life. Plus, you'll be a lousy role model for your kids.

Here is what the experts tell us about fitness. The American College of Sports Medicine (ACSM) updated their guidelines for exercise in 2007. Their recommendation went from three days a week of moderate cardiovascular exercise to five days a week of moderate cardiovascular exercise, or three days a week of vigorous cardiovascular exercise plus two weekly sessions of weight training. For the average person going through a divorce, the ACSM guidelines may become just another source of stress. Then again, it could be the ideal stress-buster! Be realistic about what you can do and check to see what your doctor recommends.

The Surgeon General's Office suggests adding walking to your daily activities, starting with just 10 minutes a day, three days a week. They suggest that you build up to walking 30 minutes, five days a week. The nice thing about the Surgeon General's recommendation is that you can split up your walking through the day. In other words, if you park far away from the store you are entering, that five-minute walk counts towards your 30 minutes a day. This plan also suggests doing something you enjoy, such as dance, yoga, or martial arts. Any physical activity counts, and if you enjoy it you will be more likely to continue doing it.

I've heard a million excuses from my patients about how they can never find the time to do any more than walk from the parking lot to my office. I smile and ask them to be more honest, not with me, but with themselves. I ask them one more thing. Why would you come to me to take care of your mind and your soul but then ignore your body? We are simply fooling ourselves to think that we can live healthy lives that way. So let me do the same with you, right now. Are you doing all that you can to be healthy? Are you even doing half of what's possible each day?

If you aren't already taking good care of yourself, now is the time to begin. But before you do, see your doctor. Make sure you have no issues holding you back.

A special thanks to Pamela Tinkham, MSW, a
psychotherapist and fitness trainer, for her kind
assistance with this chapter.

Ten Tips to Get Fit

1. **Be honest about your current state of affairs.** If you do too much too soon, you may risk injury. Newcomers to regular exercise are often in a big hurry to make changes and don't always take the time to insure that they are exercising properly.

2. **Begin with a commitment.** Work out every day and every little bit counts. Shoot for at least 30 minutes each day, and if you need to, you can intersperse your workouts throughout the day. And don't forget: warm up and cool down!

3. **Create realistic expectations.** Thinking you will look better after a few days is kind of silly, and that type of thinking can lead to overtraining, burnout, and/or injury. Go slow and be steady.

4. **Don't settle for easy goals.** Even if you're new to exercising, challenge yourself! Choose activities that are appropriate for your current fitness level (and fun). Gradually increase the intensity and duration. If you stick with it, you will see results. That's when the real fun kicks in.

5. **Use a journal to record your development.** While you're at it, you may even want to jot down your feelings. Aerobic exercise releases chemical endorphins, and they can give you quite a buzz! I often get new ideas for my work while working out on an elliptical machine.

6. **Select a workout you enjoy.** Do what you like, not what someone on TV says is right for you.

7. **Find a partner.** Organize specific times to meet and get MOVING! Try tennis, hiking, swimming, yoga—whatever works for the two of you. As long as you're moving and getting your heart rate up to speed, it's all good. If you can't find a friend at the right time, try securing yourself a personal trainer.

8. **Develop a total fitness plan.** Include aerobic conditioning, weight lifting, and flexibility training. Aerobic movement develops stamina and improves your cardio-vascular system. Weight bearing exercise can slow down osteoporosis. Increased flexibility will prevent injuries and help you sleep better.

9. **Begin with low-impact activities.** If you are overweight, or just facing an expiration date on your joints, then try swimming, cycling or walking. Take it easy. Fitness is fluid.

10. **Consider fitness as your new lifestyle.** Integrate walks, hikes, or gardening into your daily life. You can work up a good sweat without going to the gym. Hint: try the stairs instead of the elevator, and walking to your daily routine.

Please Note

If you think you have a medical condition of any kind, it is a good idea to consult a health-care provider before beginning an exercise program.

Alicia's Story

I speed walk with my iPod every evening after dinner and I highly recommend it. But why not take it a step further, so to speak? How about bringing a microcassette recorder along and while you keep a brisk walking pace you practice what you want to say to your ex-spouse, or to your lawyer, or your kids, or even questions to ask your doctor about walking too fast!. Think and move at the same time! What a concept.

Alicia, age 55

Resistance to Working Out

Just like people make excuses for eating poorly, there seems to be no shortage of reasons people use to avoid exercise and getting fit.

"I'm busy. Who has time for that kind of thing? I have to drive my kids to school, and then to work, and once I leave the office and drive home, I'm way too tired."

"Are you kidding? I can't exercise right now. I'm too stressed!"

"How do you expect me to go to a gym looking like this? I'm too fat. When I lose some weight, I'll buy a nice leotard and start exercising."

The first two people are headed for their local emergency room. The last one is on a slow, comic train to some kind of self-induced purgatory. We've all heard these classic excuses for remaining stuck with bad habits. But who actually benefits from this kind of behavior? It's not the doctors you're forced to visit because your health is failing. While they are certainly compensated for their service, I don't know any health-care professionals who really want to see divorcing people ignoring their own health. Just like with good eating habits, it's your choice to exercise and give yourself the chance to be healthy. It's also your responsibility to be the best you can be for your kids.

Let dinner wait a few minutes and take a walk once you get home from work. And, do yourself a favor when you're stressed. You'll be pleasantly surprised by how easily physical activity can calm you down. Last but not least, don't wait until you fit into some shiny, sexy leotard. Get some comfortable sweats and start moving!

Yoga

America is currently exploding with opportunities to learn and practice yoga. You'd be surprised where studios and schools are popping up. It's not just in big cities and university towns. You can find yoga classes in firehouses, bingo halls, and shopping malls. If you want to pursue yoga, which we highly recommend, it's best to find a class under the supervision of an experienced and motivating teacher. You never know what new friends you might make there, too.

You may recognize the names of a few types of yoga that are currently popular, such as Bikram, Kripalu, and Vinyasa. Bikram yoga is a series of poses done in an over-heated studio, usually between 95 and 105 degrees. This yoga should be done by those who have permission from their doctors. Practitioners claim that it helps with "detoxification" and can increase flexibility while decreasing your chances for injury. This is one of the most intense practices because of the heat and the work required to stay in a pose under these conditions. The most incredible shower of your life will be after you finish a Bikram yoga class.

Kripalu is the yoga of consciousness. There are more meditations involved in this practice and the focus is on inner awareness. Kripalu yoga is a good place to begin for the novice and a wonderful way to diminish anxiety.

Perhaps the most popular form of yoga offered today is Vinyasa yoga, which, instead of holding poses at length, concentrates on creating a flow of movement from pose to pose that is designed to keep the heart rate elevated. Vinyassa yoga also meets the ACSM guidelines for aerobic activity.

Taking Charge of Sleep

If you're reading this book, then your divorce is probably stressful, and you may be feeling some version of anxiety, depression, and chronic worry. All of these emotions can be soothed by slumber. The brain needs time to recuperate just like a sore muscle needs to heal. Sleep does the trick sometimes and its importance can't be overestimated.

"Sleep appears necessary for our nervous systems to work properly," reports the National Institute of Neurological Disorders and Stroke (2007). They also say that "without sleep, neurons may become so depleted in energy or so polluted with byproducts of normal cellular activities that they begin to malfunction. Sleep also may give the brain a chance to exercise important neuronal connections that might otherwise deteriorate from lack of activity."

If you don't get enough sleep, you may be more at risk for diabetes, obesity, and sleep apnea, all of which are associated with cardiovascular disease (Centers for Disease Control and Prevention, 2007b).

It's no secret that sleep is tough to get when you're stressed out. A tired brain yields a tired mind, which means a higher likelihood of doing or saying something you might regret. Especially during a divorce, that is something you want to avoid. So what can you do? Try to maintain a regular schedule and get the rest you require. You're not much use to anyone if you're exhausted or sick.

Dr. Randy Wright, a noted neurologist from Houston, Texas, and the co-author (with David Tabatsky) of *The Wright Choice: Your Family's Prescription for Healthy Eating, Modern Fitness, and Saving Money* (InTouch Media Health Network 2011), shares some basic rules we encourage you to follow if you want to build good sleep hygiene.

Ten Tips for Getting Good Sleep

1. **Get the bedroom cool before you go to bed.** Most people sleep better if their room is dark and cool.

2. **Take a warm bath or shower before you go to bed.** The fall in body temperature signals the brain that it is time to go to sleep.

3. **Drink warm milk or some other noncaffeinated beverage before you go to bed.** Once again, the fall in body temperature from warm back to cool tells the brain it's time to sleep. If you go to the bathroom frequently at night, you should skip this tip.

4. **Develop a pre-sleep routine.** Doing your favorite relaxing activity is a good way to wind down from the day. Listening to calming music or reading are great ways to end your day.

5. **Only go to your bedroom when you are sleepy.**

6. **Do not exercise before going to bed.** Working out tends to raise the level of excitatory neuro transmitters, and in many people this can interfere with sleep.

7. **Avoid naps during the day (for adults).**

8. **No caffeine after lunch.** It tends to stay in your system and can interfere with sleep.

9. **No alcohol within six hours of sleep.** Many people feel that alcohol helps them sleep. The reality is that alcohol will put you to sleep pretty quickly. However, as it gets metabolized in the liver over the next several hours, its breakdown products tend to disrupt sleep, and you will soon be uncomfortable

and your sleep will be disrupted. So don't fall for the age-old trap of a glass of wine before you go to bed.

10. **Avoid watching TV or working with a laptop in your bed prior to going to sleep.** For sensitive people, these activities may interfere with falling asleep.

If you are still having trouble establishing a good sleep routine, you may need to try a supplement, such as melatonin, the only hormone secreted exclusively during sleep. For some people, a small, nonaddictive dose from a health-food store may

promote a good night's rest. Dosages can vary, so speak to your healthcare provider and consult our References section in the back of the book.

Sleep medicine (hypnotics) can be helpful in extreme cases when used temporarily. As a physician, I tend to avoid these agents unless we have exhausted all other options.

Conclusion

With the embellishment of mind, body, and spirit in our consciousness, let's consider writing a new love story for you—one that begins with you loving yourself. Nourishment for the heart and soul comes from thoughtful consideration about what you are putting into your body and how you take care of it. When you align the benefits of healthy food and fitness with good sleep habits, you are on the road to wellness.

Notes

This space is for you—to remember what's important, to doodle, to make plans …

CHAPTER 7

Practical Spirituality

What Spirituality Can Do

Divorce suggests a tough transition for you and your kids, but it can have spiritual meaning as well. Although some churches, synagogues, and mosques frown on divorce and leave their congregants to their own devices, most religious leaders take divorce seriously as a spiritual challenge, and many people in their communities reap the benefits of a concerned and active clergy.

It's always a welcome surprise to discover how supportive people can be. Many divorcing parents avoid going to their place of worship out of discomfort, but that is usually a mistake. As you are going through a raw but understandably human process, congregants and friends will show you the love and support you need the most. After all, this is not the first divorce they've witnessed. Your kids may also benefit from religious classes, educational opportunities, and social activities.

The Bible tells us that we are all created in the image of God. This includes you and your children and, yes, even your ex-husband or ex-wife.

The Jewish tradition emphasizes the notion of *Tikkun Olam*, the repairing of a broken world, wherever it may be and however it has come to be that way. Similar teachings exist in Christianity and Islam which each have a strong tradition of medicine and healing.

All three faiths call on us to make the world a better place. Even in the worst of circumstances you can begin by making things better in your own private world.

Whether you follow a religious path or not, there are spiritual lessons to help you during a divorce, leading you to a deeper understanding of yourself and offering a better chance to heal.

Remember: there is life after divorce.

Meditation and Prayer

Meditation is a simple technique that has been around for ages. It's about centering yourself, clearing your mind, and being in the present moment. You find grounding in your breath, in your body, and in your connectedness to the earth. When you meditate, you settle down and foster a mindfulness to carry with you throughout your day.

There are different schools of meditation. Some are formally Buddhist while others are more western. You don't have to believe in God in order to meditate, although many people mediate with God in mind. While the practice may help you feel close to your creator, meditation is not really about asking for help or posing life questions. It is more concerned with experiencing a calm that connects you to something grounded and eternal. And for many, that by itself can provide spiritual guidance.

Dr. John Kabat-Zinn, author of *Wherever You Go There You Are,* and Dr. Herbert Benson, noted for his book *The Relaxation Response,* have provided evidence to show that meditation is a useful way to manage stress. It has been scientifically proven to reduce blood pressure, to pacify chronic anxiety, and to help people feel better when they are worried.

A review of 20 studies (spanning more than 1600 participants) found that Mindfulness-Based Stress Reduction, a secular form of meditation, helps people handle distress and disability and enhances physical and mental well-being (Grossman, Neimann, Schmidt, & Walach, 2004). Research also suggests that when you know how you'd like to act in a situation, meditation may be able to help you break free from patterned responses (Wenk-Sormaz, 2005), such as mind looping and red braining.

The practice of meditation can be integrated into your spiritual life, too. Rabbi Aryeh Kaplan writes about weaving the technique into Jewish life (*Jewish Meditation: A Practical Guide*). The Dalai Lama talks about meditation and Buddhist life (*Stages of Meditation*), and Thomas Merton discusses this practice in Christianity (*Spiritual Direction and Meditation*).

Wachholtz and Pargament (2008) claim that their study on migraines discovered that subjects who engaged in spiritual meditation (versus secular meditation) experienced fewer headaches and a greater ability to withstand them when they occurred. In addition, while meditation in general reduced negative effects and anxiety in the subjects, spiritual meditation did so to a greater extent.

Meditating works, no matter what form of its practice you choose.

On the following pages, you will be introduced to a simple progression of meditation practices, presented by Rory Pinto, a spiritual healer and meditation specialist from New York City and the founder of *Inner Resources*. Our thanks to Rory, for making meditation accessible to everyone. We highly encourage you to give it a try. But be patient. You may not experience immediate results, but soon enough, its benefits will reveal themselves.

When I was nine years old I found a book on Zen meditation, or you can say it found me. I really couldn't understand what I was reading, but I liked to look at the man sitting in meditation. I sensed a state of peace there, and felt 'I want that.' This was my beginning.

Rory Pinto

Tuning into the Basics

Before each meditation practice, take a moment to check your state of being.

> *Close your eyes and begin to observe how you are in this moment.*
>
> *Notice the state of your body, where there are sensations, and what they are like.*
>
> *Notice where there is feeling and where there is little or none.*
>
> *Notice where there is warmth or cold. Notice the state of your mind. Is there clarity?*
>
> *Fuzziness? Something in between? Name that state.*
>
> *Now notice the state of your emotions.*
>
> *What are you feeling in this moment? What are you having difficulty feeling?*
>
> *Feel whatever you are feeling. Notice what has changed in your overall state of being.*
>
> *Notice what has remained the same.*
>
> *Notice the effect of bringing awareness to your condition.*

This kind of play is our first meditation, and happiness just arises, not from what we are doing, but from how we are. As our idle thoughts cease, peace and well-being enter. Whenever we devote ourselves fully to something or someone, we are already meditating. Activities that take a degree of concentration, like golf and needlepoint, are popular because they remind us of this state. No matter what the activity is, it is the quality of our connection to it that is important. Meditation develops this ability to connect deeply with anything or anyone.

The calm, happy state of heightened awareness that comes in meditating is actually the natural state of your being. Children experience this state spontaneously. Just watch how a child focuses on something he or she loves.

Meditation is a process of focusing on one thing at a time. It's like trying to get good reception on your cell phone, only this time it's you you're tuning. Meditation trains your body, mind, and emotions to work together. When this occurs, the more in tune you become, and the static, interference, and fuzziness in your life will begin to disappear. You will find that you have more energy, and feel happier.

To assist this process, take time to check into your state of being before and after each practice. Without changing anything, just close your eyes. Begin to observe how you are in this moment.

Thoughts to Ponder and Practice

Before you can change any condition, you first have to become aware of it. Then you have a choice of what to change, and what to leave. Without your conscious awareness, any condition will tend to repeat or maintain itself automatically.

As you tune in to your comfort level, you will know the degree of change that you can handle, and you will not proceed too far or too fast. Like eating in a balanced way, you can take in only so much at one time, and you have to allow time for digestion and assimilation before you can take in any more. Notice how you speed up or slow down the process of change.

A key to facilitating this lies in allowing change to happen in its own way, at its own pace, rather than forcing the method and speed. You lead by following, making moment-to-moment corrections to your course by staying aware, by literally staying in touch. As soon as any forcing enters the process, a conflict is created and your body becomes tense. Your job is just to keep watching your own process of unfolding, and love yourself in whatever state you find yourself!

A Mini-Meditation

Begin by really feeling your feet on the floor.

As you continue feeling your feet, add a sensation: the feeling of clothes on your skin.

Realize the feeling of the air playing on your hands and face.

Now, include the feeling of the weight of your body on the chair.

Watch the rising and falling of your breath, without having to fix or change anything.

Notice whether it is long or short, deep or shallow, smooth or ragged.

Using your sense of touch, feel your body as a whole. Feel it all at once.

Feel your body having weight, taking up space, having density, and all these sensations.

While still feeling your body with all its sensations, let the listening run out

and let it hold all of the sounds in the environment for a while, near and far,

not clinging to any one sound, not pushing any sound away.

This mini-meditation (one to three minutes) is best done before and after an activity. It helps you to focus before you begin, and regroup after you have completed it. When practiced throughout the day this pause will refresh you and prevent the build-up of tension and fatigue. By bringing your awareness out of your thoughts and into your body, the practice helps to integrate your mental state with your physical state. The calmness and strength that arise allow ease, poise, and efficiency to come into your work and play.

The Mindfulness of Breathing

As you breathe, focus on the sensations you feel in the triangular area formed by the point between your eyes, the sides of your nose, and your top lip.

Watch the rise and fall of your breath, almost as if you were "being breathed."

Keep your focus on the sensations in this triangle and note the full passage of each in-breath and out-breath, from beginning to end.

Don't follow the breath into your lungs or out into the air.

Just notice the subtle sensations of the breath as it comes and goes in this area.

This mindfulness of breathing is a basic concentration practice.

It brings rest to your mind and body.

When the mind wanders or is distracted, bring your focus back to the sensations that you experience as you breathe.

Don't try to control the breath. Just watch it. Slow or fast, deep or shallow;

*what matters is not the quality of the breath, but the
quality of your attention.*

*When you are comfortable, begin to scan your body
and become aware of any physical sensations you
may encounter.*

Go to one sensation at a time, feel it and take it in.

Stay neutral: neither clinging to it nor pushing it away.

*Work down your body with awareness and experience
each sensation.*

Let it go and move on to the next one.

*Once you have scanned the entire body, begin at the
head and be aware of any sensations that you may
encounter. Include any emotions that you may
come upon.*

Focus on one sensation or feeling at a time.

*Give it a name if you wish, and move on to the next
one. As you become aware of each sensation, feeling,
or thought, bring love and kindness to it.*

Insight meditation develops the ability to experience our human processes of thinking, emoting, and sensing with detachment and compassion. The practice of witnessing from a neutral state, and loving whatever we watch opens up our perception and affects how we respond. We are no longer swept away by every thought, sensation, or feeling that comes to us, and we can act with calm and clarity.

We begin to experience thoughts, feelings, and sensations as movements, rather than as anything permanent. We learn to observe this transience first-hand, within our own bodies, and we give up trying to prolong, resist, or otherwise keep them from changing. Like an unmoving axle connected to a wheel, we watch while everything else turns.

As a result, we build a tolerance for whatever comes into our experience, and we can respond from choice, rather than react from urgency or desperation. When we are no longer afraid of, or attached to, our thoughts, feelings, or sensations, we can allow them to go on just as they are, without having to force them to be different.

The paradox is that when we accept them, they can change. Resisting them just keeps them in place. This releases the tremendous burden of feeling like we have to control everything. In letting go we are able to respond with poise, kindness, and effectiveness. By learning to witness our processes and love ourselves in whatever state we are in, we experience a new freedom.

Standing Meditations

Stand relaxed, with your knees slightly bent, legs shoulder-width apart, and your hands at your sides. Allow your fingers to gently curve and remain slightly apart.

Drop your shoulders and elbows.

Let your arms hang loosely.

Relax your hips and belly.

Your weight should be evenly balanced between front and rear, and from side to side.

Your tailbone is tipped slightly forward.

Your tongue is touching the roof of your mouth, behind your teeth.

Your eyes are looking forward and slightly down.

Imagine a line coming from the sky attached to a point in the top center of your head (on line with the tips of the ears).

Keep your posture erect and balanced, without being rigid or floppy.

Imagine this line continuing down the center of your body and connecting to a round sphere of light a little larger than a golf ball.

This sphere is at a level of two inches below your navel, sitting right in front of the spinal column. This is a reservoir for your subtle energy, called the Tantien.

Imagine that, like a puppet, your whole body is suspended from your head.

Feel yourself sinking down, relaxing, as you hang from the string.

Breathe calmly and naturally. Exhale completely and allow your chest to drop.

Let the feeling of standing in this relaxed, alert way sink in.

Stand quietly, for up to five minutes.

As simple as this practice appears, it will quickly expose your level of nervous tension, how high-strung you are, and any difficulty you may have in relaxing. It is very humbling. You will find that as you practice your nervous system will settle down and become more calm, laying a foundation for a deeper connection with yourself and a better relationship with others.

The Tao of Divorce

We know that it's always good to be calm in the middle of a storm. We also realize that detaching yourself from all the "small stuff" during a divorce will probably keep you much better focused on the bigger, more important picture. Finally, everyone's familiar with the phrase "pick your battles." All three of these ideas make good sense. The problem is, each of them can be elusive and hard to maintain, especially in the midst of a contentious, ongoing conflict, such as divorce.

That's where meditation can be your trusted ally. You can begin to reap the rewards of these principles by simply making the effort.

Prayer

Some people use meditation as a launching pad for prayer, but the two are fundamentally different. Meditation is characterized by a desire to free oneself from thinking in order to just be, while prayer is characterized by an intention to be close to God.

Meditation and prayer do share much in common, though; the very routine of showing up for and engaging in prayer is arguably meditative. Monks used to retreat to the desert for solitary meditation and prayer, and monasteries still exist today in remote places (St. Catherine's Monastery, for example, in the middle of the Sinai desert). There is also an ancient tradition in the Judeo-Christian world of meditative prayer. You might want to read *Everything Starts from Prayer: Mother Teresa's Meditations on Spiritual Life for People of All Faiths,* by Anthony Stern, M.D.

For most people, prayer is about having a meaningful connection with their Creator, and they go about this in a variety of ways. They may praise God, ask for guidance, wisdom, and healing, or engage His presence for comfort. There are as many intentions in prayer as there are emotions, all with the underlying belief that your prayers can be heard and, in some way, answered.

Your divorce isn't arbitrary; there is meaning to be found in every life-changing experience. You may use this time in your life to reassess how you can live better. What traits and circumstances contributed to the undoing of your marriage? Were you impulsive and unfaithful? Did you ever really love her? Were you more interested in how he supported the family than in loving him properly? Do you have an addiction or an untreated psychiatric problem that she couldn't live with anymore? Were you simply too passive? Look for strength in your prayer life to deal with some hard truths and commit yourself to becoming a better person. This is religion at its best.

Unhappy people may claim that the breakup of their family is divine punishment for something they did wrong. I am not so sure. While it is certainly true that divorce is a natural consequence of two people mishandling a relationship, it is theologically questionable whether it is a punishment from up high. My understanding is that spiritual traditions, at their best, depict a loving God. Human beings, on the other hand, are fully capable of creating their own pain. Our Creator is there to help us learn, pick up the pieces, and move on.

Prayer and spirituality promote self-respect and personal growth, and they each offer comfort. It's reassuring to feel that you're never alone and to know that you can communicate with your Maker. This reassurance can, in and of itself, be considered part of God's answer.

Frequent praying, meditative prayer characterized by reflection and quiet thinking, and prayer that promotes insight and inspiration, have been shown to promote psychological well-being (Maltby, Lewis, and Day, 2008). Studies also consistently document the link between religious involvement and a greater life-span (McCullough, Hoyt, Larson, Koenig, and Thoresen, 2000).

> ## Did You Know?
>
> Research indicates that various religious practices have consistent beneficial associations with health. Benefits include reduced mortality, better physical health, reports of improved quality of life, and less mental illness and drug abuse in those who practice these behaviors
> *Linda K. George. (In Jonas and Crawford, 2003)*

Prayer with Intention

Prayer becomes powerful because of the intent behind it. When going through the stress of divorce, you will be saying different things to God depending on your mood or what happened on a particular day that needs healing. This may include prayers of praise, prayers of thanksgiving, prayers for wisdom, prayers for protection, prayers for healing, prayers for forgiveness and many others.

Take a look at this small sample of prayers gathered from different traditions. What intentions are meaningful to you when you think about connecting to God?

Prayer for Forgiveness

"O Allah, forgive my sins, make my home accommodating, And grant me abundance in my livelihood.[1]

---

[1] *www.islam.tc/Dua/*

Prayer for Protection
"O Lord, grant that this night we may sleep in peace,
and that in the morning our awakening may also be in peace.
May our daytime be cloaked in your peace.
Protect us and inspire us to think and act only out of love.
Keep far from us all evil.
May our paths be free from all obstacles from
when we go out until we return home."[2]

Prayer for Wisdom
"Great is the wisdom of the Lord!
God Almighty, Your Wisdom includes an
understanding of what is fair,
What is logical, what is true, what is right and what is lasting.
It mirrors Your pure intellect!
I entreat You to grant me such Wisdom, that
my labors may reflect Your insight.
Your Wisdom expands in Your creations,
displaying complexity and multiplicity.
Your Wisdom is an eternity ahead of man.
May Your wisdom flourish forever!"[3]

Prayer of Thanksgiving
For each new morning with its light,
for rest and shelter of the night,
for health and food, for love and friends,
for everything Thy goodness sends.[4]

---

[2] from the Babylonian Talmud / *www.godweb.org/PrayersJewish.htm*
[3] *www.catholic.org/prayers/prayer.php?p=1182*
[4] Ralph Waldo Emerson

What Children Can Teach Us About Prayer

Children know how to play. They also know how to pray. It comes naturally to them because they are free and open to the notion that they are not alone, and that there is a God in the universe who cares. We adults can learn so much about prayer by understanding our kids.

While some may disagree, I believe that the human mind is a gift from God, a vehicle for the connection between us and our maker. Yet as we grow older and become encrusted with daily life and habituated to the miracle of existence, the mind serves to constrict that connection.

Kids teach us to open up to life and to God. And that is what prayer is, at its core: a call for the experience of presence. When you feel distant from faith, it is difficult to evoke the experience of God by your side as you pray. When you have freed yourself to your faith, there is a higher likelihood of obtaining a sense of the divine in your life.

Not all traditions require a living God in order to pray, and in these traditions (Ethical Cultural, Buddhists, among others) prayer evokes a sense of being that quiets the mind in the midst of everyday chaos. But in the deistic faiths, the presence of the divine can be quite personal and dear. In the midst of a divorce, an adult with a childlike openness can find herself transported to a place of reassurance and wisdom that is worth the effort.

The Power of Community

Most human beings benefit from an ongoing relationship with a group that is larger than they are. This may be one reason why people who regularly attend church or synagogue live longer and experience less stress. In fact, a recent study analyzing data from 22 European countries found that men and women who *never* attended services were more likely to report poor health than those who did (Nicholson, Rose, and Bobak, 2010).

Divorce can become so isolating. You are busy and stressed, and your kids need supervision. This may be a good time to go to church or to join a group. I can recall a few men who joined a theater company during the throes of their divorce, providing them with community and great fun during a tough time. On the more therapeutic end of the spectrum, Alcoholics Anonymous (AA) can be a marvelous group for people with chemical dependency problems.

You may find support in a prayerful community, at work, with friends and family, or with a community of divorcees who want to form friendships with you because your experiences are similar. If one community doesn't work for you, keep looking. Don't indulge your regressive thoughts and allow yourself to feel like a pariah. There are people who will listen, and the physical and mental health benefits are too great to pass up. Perhaps the best source for a support group in your area can be found by contacting DivorceCare, a national network of divorce support groups (*www.divorcecare.com*).

Some community activities include book clubs, hiking groups, going out with "the girls" (or "the boys"), joining the PTA, taking a dance class (or pottery or cooking), or going to the local gym.

For better and for worse, in the twenty-first century, you don't have to necessarily find community in person. There are many websites devoted to helping divorcing individuals communicate with each other, like *www.fristwivesworld.com, www.divorcenetwork.com,* and *HuffPost.com/divorce.*

Many divorced people also enjoy dating sites, not just in order to meet romantic partners, but also to seek the platonic company of like-minded men and women. They flirt, they talk, they share their woes, and in a way it's one big connection. It can backfire because people don't always present themselves truthfully, but I've seen many people enjoy plugging in to websites such as *www.match.com*, *www.JDate.com*, *www.spark.com*, and *www.eHarmony.com*.

Finally, Facebook is becoming a meeting place for adults who want to reconnect to old friends and buddies or even past romantic interests. Just like with dating sites, this is an opportunity, but it carries risks. Things you say about your life or about your ex are forever sealed in the digital universe. Be cautious because something said online can be used against you in a court of law.

At the end of the day, very little good is derived from sitting in your living room waiting for something to happen. Be appropriately cautious about online communities. See if you can handle the power of a cyber-community and be aware of the risks. Through a bit of trial and error, figure out what works for you and go for it!

Notes

This space is for you—to remember what's important, to doodle, to make plans ...

Part Three

Secure, Strong, and Hopeful

A Call to Action: Children, Money and Health

At some point during the course of a divorce, you may consider yourself a failure at the one thing you wanted more than anything: a loving marriage, a stable family and a warm home. You naturally worry about the children, money and what the future holds for you. Even worse, you may be haunted by the feeling that your children have lost the only "home" they have known.

Do not despair. Despite the pressures, the most difficult effects of divorce tend to recede once you pass through its beginning and middle phases. Stay positive, and remember that a house doesn't make a home; people do. You have the power to take charge of the situation and become a role model for your kids. But it takes a daily commitment to positive behavior.

Ask yourself a few questions. Does this divorce have to overwhelm everybody? Do my children have to constantly worry? Do they really need to know most of what is going on?

The answer is no, no, and no. Your first responsibility is simply to be there for your kids, actively engaged in their daily lives. If both parents can remain involved in a healthy way, that's great; but at least one of you has to.

And what better place to begin than at home? You have learned how to protect the Intergenerational Boundary, manage power struggles, and become a better role model. This should give you the confidence to tackle a few other issues.

In Chapter 8, you will learn more about child and adolescent development, including what can go wrong and what you can do about it.

In Chapter 9, we will address your financial well-being because taking charge of your finances will help you feel more secure. It's especially targeted for single parents, adjusting to new financial territory. This can mean figuring out how you feel about money, and focusing on short and long term planning. For example, if you intend to stay in the marital home, can you swing it without a second income? If it's a new place, is the mortgage or rent realistic? Beyond the dwelling itself, what happens when you look in the desk drawer that holds your checkbook and portfolio? Are you at ease? Can you sleep okay at night, without mind looping about money?

We'll come full circle in Chapter 10, focusing once again on taking care of yourself with an action plan designed for you. Take good care of the one thing you have control over: your body, health and well-being. Take an active interest by recording your progress. When you do well, your children will benefit.

CHAPTER 8

When Kids Regress: Signs and Solutions

Your Pride and Joy

How well do you really know your own children and their developing personalities? Sure, they're cute and fun when they're little, exasperating and challenging as they grow, and astonishing and nerve-racking as they mature into young adults. At any age, they're your pride and joy. But they're not always so easy to understand.

For those of you who studied Early Child Education in college or have ever worked with children, some things may be familiar. However, for many parents, a simple primer in basic child development might come in handy, especially during a divorce, when it can be helpful to draw on some basic knowledge to assist you in understanding your children. That way, you will feel better equipped to parent them in the way they deserve. Preserving their innocence is our goal, and educating ourselves about who they are is a big step toward accomplishing that.

Don't Blink—They Grow Too Fast!

Consider the basic developmental curve and milestones most children follow from birth through their teenage years. When things appear to be going haywire with your kids, it may not have anything to do with your divorce. It may very well just be a case of children being themselves.

As children move through various stages of development, they face a certain amount of risk. For example, when a child is born, and for approximately its first three years, they develop a basic trust in the world, defining what is safe and what may be not. At the same time, some children may experience inconsistent schedules, which can increase separation anxiety or produce sleeping issues. Between the ages of four and seven, as children develop imaginative skills and experience cognitive shifts, they may also encounter fear, depression, nightmares, and a host of other difficult emotions. During more advanced school years, as kids acquire social skills and enter adolescence, they are at risk for identity issues, academic challenges, and varying degrees of conflict with their parents.

Naturally, there are exceptions to all of these tendencies, but learning about your child's developmental tasks, risks, and symptoms can benefit every parent. If you have any questions, ask your pediatrician, school nurse, or a child psychologist.

Please Note:

In *The Intelligent Divorce—Book One: Taking Care of Your Children,* we discuss your children's development in greater depth.

What to Watch Out For

Naturally, children become more vulnerable during a divorce, and it's imperative that you understand the nature of their changing behavior when they are being placed at risk.

For instance, kids regress. While they may be doing fine in some aspects of their development (ability to be alone, capacity to self-direct, ability to handle academics), their behavior can also become quite uneven. Under stress, many kids fall back into patterns consistent with a younger age. These ebbs and flows are normal at many stages of development but may become accentuated under the pressures divorce can present.

Everyone's entitled to bad days. It's important to watch out for questionable behavior without, at the same time, succumbing to knee-jerk reactions you may later regret. Bad days don't necessarily indicate significant psychological problems. For example, in the midst of your divorce your ten-year-old son begins to occasionally wet his bed. This alone is probably not a reason for alarm. He's entitled to a moment of regression here and there. If, on the other hand, this becomes a daily occurrence, then you'll need to consult your pediatrician.

Brushing up on the basics of child development will help you recognize what's happening with your child, and what you may need to do to help her.

We've explained the consequences of power struggles and how the stress of a divorce can affect you and your children. The first book in our series deals entirely with the subject of children and divorce, but because it's so important and because you play such a large role in determining how they get through this process, we will touch on it here as well.

Some kids handle divorce quite well, with little emotional upset or acting out. Others are overwhelmed by sadness, fear,

213

or confusion, or get roped into their parents' battle. Kids grieve, too. You may have lost your marriage and the family you anticipated having, but they have lost a sense of stability. Things will never quite be the same for them, and because they're young, their defenses are less developed, making them more vulnerable.

Children will regress (it's not a matter of if), and they will be affected. While they may be doing fine in some aspects of their development, their behavior can also be quite uneven. These ebbs and flows are normal at many stages of growth, but they may become accentuated under the pressures of divorce.

Signs

Like adults, children and teenagers can suffer from any number of psychological disorders. Generally, these include:

1. Attention Disorders
2. Anxiety Disorders
3. Behavioral Disorders
4. Chemical Dependency or Addiction
5. Mood Disorders
6. Eating Disorders

As we mentioned, you can find a more comprehensive list of disorders in the back of this book, but you don't need this list to tell you that something is wrong. Take a look at the following examples, illustrating some of the ways that children can struggle during a divorce.

EXAMPLE
Not As "Perfect" As She Looks

Erin, a ten-year-old girl, was into everything. She would annoy her older brother, couldn't stop talking, and was a terror to her younger sister—the average middle-child syndrome.

When her parents divorced, Erin's personality changed. She started asking her mother what she could do to help her younger sister. Her older brother no longer found her provocative. She completed her homework without complaint and she helped her mom organize the house. She even set the table occasionally.

"From the Couch"

Erin has morphed from an unruly child into a perfect one. This might seem great: after all, who doesn't want her to mature and to be more responsible?

The problem is that Erin's changes aren't a consequence of her natural development—they can be traced to a definite source: the breakup of her family.

Erin has become "perfect" in order to compensate for the instability she feels around her. She thinks that if she is good, her world will improve. Maybe Mom and Dad will get back together. At the very least, she hopes that Mom will stop crying so much and that Dad will come around more often.

Erin is anxious, and she needs help to get back on a healthy developmental course. She'll stop riling up her brother and sister at some point in her life—but right now, she should be able to enjoy her middle-child role. You can let her know that no one is perfect and no one needs to be, either.

EXAMPLE
The Oppositional Child

Leo is the youngest of three children. He is always pleasant, but his parents' divorce has upset him; he simply doesn't do what is asked of him. He lives with his mother and visits his father regularly.

"Leo, turn the TV off!" his mom cries out.

"No!" Leo barks back.

"Leo, it's time!"

"No!"

"I'm going to unplug it!"

"If you do that, I'll tell Daddy!"

A few nights later, at Leo's dad's house, a similar event occurs.

"Leo, it's time for bed," his dad announces.

"Later, I'm not tired."

"Leo, it's time."

"I'm thirsty! Give me a second!"

"Leo, I said it's time for bed!"

"Don't bother me, Dad! I'll tell Mommy. You're a terrible father, you know that? Neither one of you really loves me!"

"From the Couch"

The negativity and resistance Leo displays is common in depressed children. But Leo is also angry. We don't know all the reasons why, but we can imagine he isn't happy about the divorce or about traveling between houses. His anger comes out when his parents set limits and make him transition from one thing to the next.

Oppositional Defiant Disorder (ODD) is common, even in intact families; if it continues unabated, it can lead to major problems, like conduct disorder, school failure, and addiction. These are treatable but they need to be handled early on by getting to the source of the issue and by having both parents work together as a team.

EXAMPLE
The Drug Abuser

Minda's dad left home when she was 14 years old. She hasn't seen him since, and he and her mother are officially divorced. Minda lives with her mom, who has noticed that her daughter is picking up some bad habits in school. She even suspects drug use.

One Friday night, she confronts her daughter.

"Minda, I don't want you going out tonight."

"I'm fine, Mom; leave me alone. What do you want me to do?"

"Are you using drugs?"

"No! Do you think I'm an idiot?"

"I'm just asking," her mom replies, feeling confused.

Five hours later, at two in the morning, Minda's mother wakes up and goes to her daughter's room. Minda isn't there. Frantic, the mother runs out of the apartment and takes the elevator downstairs. She sees a car parked in front of the building and finds Minda inside, getting high with someone she's never seen before.

"From the Couch"

The seeds for drug and alcohol abuse are usually planted in a person's teenage years. If others in the family struggle with addiction, it's more likely to occur, but stressful events, like divorce, can also lead vulnerable children astray. Be mindful of your child's progress in school and observe his general demeanor. If something seems unusual, don't ignore it. It's always better to catch a problem before it gets too big.

EXAMPLE
The Depressed Teenager

Colby, a 16-year-old teen, is handling his parents' divorce poorly. He used to be a fun-loving kid who did well in school and enjoyed his friends, whether on Facebook, over the phone, or by playing basketball.

Colby has grown sullen. He stays home a lot now—he would rather sleep and watch TV than play outside or go on the internet.

"Let's go to the park and shoot some hoops," his dad says to him one day, trying to coax Colby into some action.

"I'm tired," Colby replies.

"You know, some of your friends might be there. I can watch you guys play; it's okay."

"Nah, I don't think so."

"Come on Colby, we'll have fun!"

"Tomorrow, Dad, okay?"

"From the Couch"

Divorce is hard for a lot of kids. Their world changes, and even if you're the picture-perfect parent, they are probably going to have a tough time with the transition. But Colby is having more than just a hard time; he is in a funk. His isolation from his friends and his loss of interest in previously enjoyed activities are two hallmark signs indicating depression.

If you notice that your child no longer wants to go to school, has frequent headaches, or has changed her eating habits, you should probably seek advice from your pediatrician. Depression also manifests itself as moodiness—so pay careful attention to any "difficult" or "acting out" behavior your child displays.

Teens, Moodiness, and Divorce

Mood disorders are real. Common causes include breakups, divorce, death, or any sudden change in life circumstances. They are best handled in a straightforward way. Avoidance makes them worse, and honest assessment and treatment often save the day.

Mood disorders–depression, bipolarity, or a variation of the two—are more common in teenagers than we might think. Tackling the issue from a diagnostic point of view can be tricky; by default teenagers are inconsistent and moody, and they often test our limits.

So how do you tell the difference between what's normal and what's not? Any disorder is defined not just by what one experiences but also by how it impacts basic functionality. If you notice your son acting depressed, but he isn't suicidal, he does well in school, he has good friends and an active social life, and he generally gives off an attitude of contentment, you are most likely dealing with normal teenage angst. If, on the other hand, your daughter protests constantly that she's "fine" but you clearly witness her having trouble getting out of bed in the morning, her friends are no longer calling, and she has lost interest in what used to give her pleasure, this well may be an actual depression.

Evidence of extreme moodiness may be your child staying in bed for an excessively long time or going for days without showering or changing clothes, seemingly losing interest in personal appearance and grooming. Or, on the flipside, you might witness flights of manic energy, sleeplessness, and grandiosity. In these instances, you might be up against a bigger problem than mere teenage moodiness. Mood disorders can be hereditary, so educate yourself regarding the mental health history on both sides of your family. If your child is adopted, you will have to dig further to find out if the biological parents have any of these issues.

Depression and other mood disorders are treatable. If you suspect a problem you must be proactive about getting the child seen by a mental health professional. I generally recommend that parents tell their children that they're coming in for an assessment with no obligation. This lightens the load, allowing them to feel less trapped, and paradoxically, lets them open up.

If real depression, bipolar disorder, or their less severe cousins dysthymia and cyclothymia are diagnosed, treatment includes one or a combination of supportive psychotherapy, cognitive behavior therapy (CBT), and prescribed medications.

Therapy itself sometimes does the job, but at times, the mood can be so severe or longstanding that medication should be considered, even for teenagers. Many psychiatrists, including myself, will tell their patients that medication can be very effective, and that when it works, it's a godsend. When it is indicated, we medicate children in order to give them the strength to overcome the obstacles that are affecting them so that in the future they can get back on track and fare well.

Counseling Kids

Counseling is great preventative medicine, and I recommend it for every young person affected by divorce. When a child or a teenager loses the bedrock he had always counted on, he can experience denial, bargaining, anger, and depression.

Counseling allows the child's voice to be heard. It allows her to grieve. If either parent is problematic, or if there is tension, having a safe adult to confide in can relieve stress. The counselor may also be able to effect change or give the child a sense of power where he or she would otherwise feel powerless.

When moms and dads act out, therapists can teach children how to deal more effectively with their environment. A good counselor will even invite the parents to share in the process. You can never have enough people supporting your child.

Therapists don't necessarily need to dig deep; they may decide the best course is to support the development of healthy defenses, like denial. The most important thing a counselor can do is give the child a sense of mastery over his shifting world so that he can feel capable of handling major changes in the future.

Medication

When I work with a child, I think about her long-term development, not just about the kid who happens to be in the room with me at the time. What will she be like in five or 10 years? What interventions can I make that will optimize her development? What interventions can I afford *not* to make, giving therapy alone and natural growth the chance to do their jobs?

These are important questions because we want to be effective. Kids are growing organisms, and when they are on the right trajectory, their self-esteem and sense of competence develop. When they're off track, however, they can be damaged in ways that are hard to undo.

Many people are skeptical of medication, and I support the critique that they're over-prescribed in the United States. Managed care, utilization review, cost containment, pressure from pharmaceutical companies, and the desire for a quick fix, lead many doctors, school officials, or parents to the same conclusion: prescribe a drug and hope it solves the problem. It's not a great approach.

For parents who suspect that your child may have a problem, I suggest you seek a full assessment, starting with your pediatrician. He or she may recommend a psychologist or child psychiatrist to perform an evaluation, determine a diagnosis, and create a treatment plan. You should review this plan with the therapist and understand it fully.

For more information on psychological issues and their treatments, may we suggest the first book in this series, *The Intelligent Divorce: Taking Care of Your Children,* as well as a section in the back of this book, entitled Common Psychological and Personality Disorders.

Keeping It Simple

Despite our best intentions, parents and psychologists often miss the most basic things that kids in the midst of a divorce are seeking: normal, everyday stuff! When children's lives are turned upside down, it's often the simplest things that we take for granted that can settle them down and renew their faith in the world. Before you worry too much about your children, remember that there is no substitute for good parenting. Let common sense dictate.

Common Sense for Divorcing Parents

It's not always easy to figure out what's best for your kids because just when you think you know what they're up to they're moving on to another phase. But no matter what age they are, chronologically and developmentally, you must establish rules and regulations at home (in both homes, in fact) if you are to give your children a good chance of growing up healthy and happy. Because we stress the importance of protecting the innocence of your children, here are ten tried and true methods for getting through a divorce intact and well.

We're also taking the long view, projecting how your kids will benefit 10–20 years down the road from things being done well now.

Maintain a Stable Schedule

Young children need a steady schedule in order to feel comfortable. This includes knowing when it is time for bed, time to eat and time to wake up etc. Though they might disagree, even teenagers need reliable, stable environments, and they definitely still need limits.

You and your ex-spouse must work together to ensure that your child follows a reliable and constant visitation schedule, with similar customs and expectations in both of your homes. By creating a predictable schedule you will help your children develop in a positive way.

10–20 Years Later: A stable schedule in early life contributes to stability in adulthood.

A chaotic childhood may lead to a chaotically organized adult life.

Transitions

Your child will experience countless transitions as he or she matures. Even something as seemingly inconsequential as turning off the television to start homework counts as a transition for your child, as does the change from summer time to the beginning of the school year and, of course, the constant shuttling back and forth between parents' houses. Parents must help their kids negotiate these transitions successfully.

As always, *fore-warned* is *fore-armed*. Parents learn early on that most of their child's unwelcome behavioral issues occur during times of transition. Be prepared. Tell your child when dinner will be ready so she knows when she should be at the table. If your child isn't a morning person, wake him up a few minutes earlier to get ready. Communicate with your ex about any transition problems.

Be aware of how your child deals with changes and look for signs that say: "I need help." Is she leaving homework and textbooks on the table in the morning by mistake? Does he need to be woken up multiple times? Is she partying with her friends as high school nears an end to distract her from the concern of leaving home so soon? These are just a few examples of how transitions can help you realize new things about what your child is going through and use this new understanding to be a better parent.

10–20 Years Later: Handling transitions well gives a child basic trust in the world—an idea introduced by Erik Erikson, the noted developmental psychologist. When your children encode the memory of going from house to house without incident and they recollect the divorce itself as relatively benign, they believe, deep down, that whatever comes their way, they can handle. This makes them strong adults.

Quality Time

If you spend time with your kids engaging in activities that are fun for them, you will have fun, too. Get on the floor and color with your toddler, play dress-up with your seven-year-old, and tell the bedtime stories that your child enjoys. Finding new ways to relate to your children on their level enhances your relationship with them.

Real time counts. Most adults today are obsessed with their communication devices. You know, the people who can't go 30 seconds without checking their email, texting their friends, or keeping tabs on their stocks etc. Too many parents are getting more face time with an electronic device than with their own kids. Try to focus on them, doing what they like to do.

10–20 Years Later: A lot of what's important in life is non-verbal—just being there with your child teaches her that she is important. It's nice to hear the words, " I love you," but it's even better to experience the behavior of being loved. Spend a lot of good time with your kids. It'll give them the best of what you have, and they'll pass it on to their children when it's their time.

Listen to Your Kids

Playing with your kids can provide a way to problem solve with them and influence the development of a strong and adaptive ego. With a two-year-old, you can help him balance blocks more adroitly and take pleasure in discovering that once something is knocked down, it can, with some effort, be put back together. He learns about fixing things.

This is a nice lesson for a child in the midst of a divorce. While reading to your seven-year-old, you may be surprised how open she'll be about something that happened at school. With your 15-year-old, it's good to bond on her turf and perhaps shop together at the mall. You can observe and aid in her decision-making—what to buy, how much she has to spend etc. You'll be surprised how often she may open up to you, about the divorce and other things, when you're both casually walking along, doing something else, because she doesn't feel any acute pressure to confide in you at that moment.

10–20 Years Later: Did you ever have a coach, a priest, a teacher, or a parent say something that stayed with you years later? This is what you can give your children. Be with them when they have a problem, whether it's homework or something personal. Encourage them to solve it. Don't give them the answers, but instill them with confidence. This is a gift they will never forget. It will help them in business, relationships, with their own kids, and with life, in general.

Your Words Count

It's important that children are reminded every once in a while that the divorce is not their fault. Children employ their own brand of magical thinking and may assume that if they had only done something differently their parents would still be together.

"If only I had—"

Trauma commonly sparks self-doubt and questioning in adults. Imagine what it must be like for kids? Just remind them from time to time, almost in passing, that they are not responsible for Mom and Dad breaking up. Your words count. It's good to occasionally remind them that both their mom and their dad love them equally.

"I love you," is always nice, but it's relatively passive.

"I believe in you," can be the greatest source of a child's self-esteem. It's your best way of putting your love into action.

10–20 Years Later: Your adult child is not suffering from unresolved magical thinking. He isn't worried about what people think of him or pleasing everyone. He is his own man.

Books and Movies Invite Conversation

Books are great conversation starters for children of all ages. Given the statistics, it is very likely that your child knows someone in his class whose parents have gotten divorced, and chances are good that he has spoken to that child about divorce as well.

When you read about another family it's not as emotional as when you talk about yourself or your family. Once your child no longer feels the weight of her own situation, she will feel comfortable talking to you about your divorce. This will provide you with the opportunity to offer support, clear up any questions she has, and understand your child's feelings better.

Use common sense. If your child isn't a book fan, try a movie. There are many films that cover the theme of divorce in a sensitive way. Check the list in the back of this book.

10–20 Years Later: Constructive, non-toxic conversation about the divorce helps to settle your child, so he realizes that he isn't alone, that others have gone through the same thing and have fared well. Ten or 20 years later, he is a healthy adult. He has put the divorce behind him, and he feels neither stigmatized by nor ashamed of his family history.

Practice Restraint

When you talk negatively about your child's other parent you risk damaging your child's faith in the trustworthiness of the adult world. She feels caught in the middle.

Your child's innocence is hard to protect. You may feel frustrated and angry, but it's important to shield your children from that. It probably seems easy and "helpful" to let your child know some bad secrets about your ex. It's your way of telling your child: *"Do you see what I had to deal with?"* Unloading on your child is selfish and will only confuse him more.

It's also important to keep in mind that your son is not your ex-husband. You should not punish him because of your ill feelings and frustrations toward your ex-husband. Your daughter may look like her mother. She may even share some of her mannerisms. But she is not your ex. She deserves to be treated solely as your daughter, as her own person, with love and respect.

10–20 Years Later: We all know that bad news travels ten times faster than good. It's also remembered longer. You may have been an angry 30-year-old mother, but your daughter doesn't have to be burdened by your unhappiness 10 or 20 years later. If you do it right, she may still like you!

Tell the Truth

Mark Twain once said, "Always tell the truth, it is easier to remember your story that way." Divorce is something your kids will carry with them for their entire lives. As adults, they will gain new perspective on your divorce and how it affected them. When they think back to their childhood, they should remember the truths that you told them. What you tell your child is dependent upon his or her age, along with other factors, and should be the truth, within the limitations of the situation.

Your children should be protected from unnecessary information; they are still kids after all. If you don't know the best time to start talking to your child, or you are unsure about how much to share, consider talking to your pediatrician or with a specialist in child development.

When in doubt, keep quiet! Once things are said, you can't take them back.

10–20 Years Later: Don't confuse your kids. There's a lot that's just too much for them to understand. For instance, if you had a bad sex life, they probably never need to know it. By protecting your child's innocence, she gets to be a kid and enjoy the task of growing up. She will be more confident and less neurotic. Remember that she *will* remember, so let her be a kid.

Kids Should Love Both Parents

Your child deserves to experience loving two parents. While you may feel badly for your children regarding the divorce, becoming so preoccupied with your own emotional survival may mistakenly pull them into the middle of your conflict. Respect Intergenerational Boundaries.

You may hate your ex. And you may have every right to feel that way. But don't poison your son or daughter's feelings about your ex-spouse. This is particularly hard to do if you sense that he or she is doing this to you. Someone has to protect the innocence of your kids. Two wrongs don't make a right so don't ask them to choose; or keep secrets. Let your children remain children. Never use your child as a messenger between you and your ex-spouse. It's awkward for children to be put in that position; no matter how convenient it might be for you.

10–20 Years Later: When kids are forced to take both sides, they learn to please, fix, and deny when there are problems. They carry this into their adult lives, and approach all conflict similarly. This is energy depleting, and it doesn't make for happy relationships.

Feeling Guilty?

Even if your divorce is going smoothly and your kids seem to be dealing with it extraordinarily well, you will probably still feel surges of guilt for what you are putting them through. This is normal. However, when you begin to feel this way, take a step back, make yourself think and act objectively.

Discipline and structure are needed in your household. Your guilt is not an excuse to coddle your children or spoil them. They will become responsible adults if you set limits and raise the bar for what you expect of them. Some parents will lower the bar or drop it completely in order to feel loved by their kids. This may ease their guilt, but it is not a good idea and will harm your children in the long run.

10–20 Years Later: Parenting requires loving-kindness and limit setting. We love our kids to pieces but we must set limits to help them grow up. Loving a child without setting limits is like letting someone eat ice cream without eating dinner; it's unhealthy. When you've raised your kids responsibly, they'll know how to discipline themselves. They'll be capable in all they do.

Shopping together and buying your daughter everything in the mall to assuage your guilt are not the same thing.

SCRAPBOOK
WHAT MY DIVORCE HAS TAUGHT ME ABOUT MY KIDS

There is no amount of money or excitement that could replace love, safety, and security for my child.

I remarried 13 years ago and had another son with my second wife, with whom I presently live. My first son embraces his stepfamily and loves having a little brother.

ANY environment has an impact on a child. I have learned that our family situation inevitably has an impact on my child and will bring out his strengths and talents as well as placing demands upon him. I have learned that my child is a creative, adaptable, and flexible person who speaks his mind and is not afraid to express his feelings and preferences. I have learned that my child can form many deep, significant bonds with other people and is growing, learning, and thriving. This is a tremendous relief-being from a divorced family does not in and of itself damage a child. This is true as long as the parents keep the child's needs as the top priority in the co-parenting relationship.

My children love me no matter what, even when they're hating me. As hard as it is to see them making the same mistakes I made, I let them make their own mistakes. I also learned that my children do not necessarily need what I need. As Kahlil Gibran says, "They have their own needs."

It's a good thing for my son to have close relationships with other people involved in his father's life. I'm so glad I realized that and it doesn't threaten our relationship.

Neither of my kids really seemed to suffer severe consequences from the divorce. We didn't make them choose between us; we didn't downgrade the other parent; we were supportive of each other as parents, so I think that really helped. Plus they are resilient, adaptive kids.

Notes

This space is for you—to remember what's important, to doodle, to make plans ...

CHAPTER 9

A Financial Primer
for Single Parents

"How do we pay for everything once we get divorced?"

The Psychology of Money

Money can drive anyone getting a divorce to the point of distraction. It can become the biggest weapon and the worst cause of fear and insecurity. For some, it can rule the entire process. That being said, and fully realizing the psychological implications—how it can threaten your self-preservation and survival, how what he's doing just isn't fair, how she's taking advantage of you—it's time to be pragmatic and deal with the economics of your life.

An intelligent divorce demands intelligent management of your finances, and if you don't learn about it and actively take control, you put power in other people's hands. Planning for life during and after divorce includes developing a financial plan that begins with the period of divorce proceedings and looks ahead to your long-term goals for life after divorce.

Before you start calling your accountant and spending lots of money on financial planners and lawyers, it will serve you well to level with yourself about how you generally feel about money. Sure, we all want to have enough money to take care of our selves and our children, but it's important to look deeper and review our historical relationship with money.

If you examine your experience as a child and as an emerging adult you may learn something by considering how your parents dealt with financial issues. Quite often, their sensibilities shaped yours, regardless of divorce. For instance, do you or your spouse come from wealthy families? Were either of you raised on hope and a prayer? Are you embarrassed about talking about financial matters? Do you habitually spend too much? Are you willing to work hard for a certain lifestyle, or is discretionary time more important to you than owning stuff?

Answering these questions will help you understand your attitude towards money, which is also dictated by your career, your ex-spouse's situation, and the current needs of your family. Regardless of how your circumstances vary, it's good to remember, even in the midst of a contentious divorce, all that you have to be thankful for. You may have a lot of "things" to fight over, but consider all the people who started with nothing and have even less of it after a divorce. This sense of realistic gratitude, even in the midst of what could be a big loss, should inform your actions and offer moments of thanksgiving.

As you manage the inevitable maze of negotiating the division of property and assets, spousal and child support, and any other invariably surprising costs, you'll be doing yourself a huge favor if you've already thought these issues through and determined what your goals are, not only in the short and long term, but on a psychological and spiritual level as well.

Short-Term Goals

Nowadays, most judges aren't interested in the relationship between a divorcing husband and wife because there is very little they haven't heard. This may surprise you, but as long as there is a legal basis to end a marriage, they don't preoccupy themselves with who did what to whom, unless any children have been hurt in the process.

Judges are concerned about how each party and their children will move forward with their lives, and this is where finances come in. When you're splitting one household into two, there are issues of distribution (who gets what?), child support (how will we afford what the kids need?), and maintenance (does one spouse need help getting back on his or her feet?) to consider.

Before you can answer these questions, you'll need to have a clear picture of your marital estate, including your family's assets and liabilities: where they are, what form they are in, and, in the case of debts, to whom they are owed. You may not know all of this right now, and that's okay. It means that you will want to start gathering data.

The Run to the Bank

Some of you may be feeling anxious about the finances of your pending divorce, and for good reason. We all need money to live, and some of you may be quite vulnerable in that area and react out of fear. You may be afraid that you'll be left with nothing, or you may worry about your spouse draining your hard-earned savings.

> *Will my husband drain our checking account, leaving the kids and me with nothing?*
> *Is it okay to take money out of our savings, even before we're officially divorced?*
> *My lawyer is telling me to empty our account. Should I?*

When it comes to joint accounts and credit cards, a simple rule of thumb is to consult a lawyer and determine whether you are liable for any expenditures of your soon-to-be ex-spouse. At the same time, you can find out the laws of your particular state and whether or not you are entitled to withdraw half of certain monies you may jointly share.

Getting Help

Many people will want to tackle these issues on their own, and many won't be able to afford outside help, but if it's at all possible, we do recommend that you get a professional opinion.

Dividing a family's finances and getting the right support for your children, your spouse, and yourself can be dizzying. There are state requirements, taxes to consider, and issues of support and fair distribution. While you may be capable of figuring all of this out, it's a good idea to talk to a professional who has done it hundreds of times. It's too much work and it's too important to do alone.

If you use a mediator, she will help you determine your financial settlement; that is her job. If you use a collaborative lawyer or a traditional matrimonial attorney, he will also advise you on how to assess the marital estate. In addition, he will argue the case on your behalf.

Other professional players include forensic accountants, who determine where money may be hidden, and financial planners. Meeting with an attorney is a good place to start.

Determining the Marital Estate

Ascertaining the complete net worth and liabilities of a marriage requires some legwork. A good place to begin is with your bank statements and tax returns. Your attorney may ask you to bring them in for him to see. It's also helpful to take a good look at your household's income streams. Are you both earning money? Do you receive income from sources outside of employment, like Social Security?

Most states require the submission of sworn statements attesting to each partner's assets and liabilities, and this is another great starting point. These forms typically ask for family data: presence and age of kids, type of employment, educational background, and monthly expenses (housing, utility, food, clothing, medical, household help, recreational). To document your assets, you will include information on your income, pension plans, checking and savings accounts, real estate, and investments. Liabilities are all about owing money, so you'll want to know whether you have any credit card debt. If you are carrying a home equity line of credit, you'll want to know who holds the mortgage.

If you're not sure where to go for this data, here is a suggested list of documents whose review may prove helpful. It's not necessarily a complete list by any means, but it's a good start.

- Bank statements
- Credit card statements
- Life insurance policy statements
- Mortgage and brokerage house statements
- Real estate documents
- Personal and business tax returns

Gathering all of this information together may be a hassle, and you've certainly got enough on your mind, but it serves an important purpose. Once you know where your household stands financially, you can start deciphering what is yours from what you and your ex hold together. These are called *separate* and *marital* assets; identifying them is a prerequisite to the fair resolution of economic issues and to the equitable distribution of the marital estate.

> ## Did You Know?
>
> **Equitable Distribution** is the distribution of a marital estate. This includes the assets and liabilities a couple has acquired. "Equitable" does not mean equal, but the longer a marriage lasts, the more likely the distribution will, in fact, be equal.

Separate versus Marital Assets

Marital property is usually defined as property acquired by either party during the marriage and before the commencement of the divorce action. States often define separate property as property held by either person prior to the marriage or acquired from property owned separately during the marriage (if that property maintained its separate identity), or if it was acquired during the marriage by inheritance or gift.

At first glance, it may seem relatively easy to separate what is uniquely yours and what is uniquely your partner's and, in some cases, it is. If you each owned a car before your marriage, your car will probably remain yours. If you bought and moved into an apartment together after you were married, it's likely that the apartment will be considered joint property. But what if you purchased a house before your marriage and your husband, who moved in after the wedding, helped you maintain it and pay for upgrades? His actions have contributed to your home's increase in value, and he can probably now claim a piece of it.

Inevitably, your marital estate will consist of some of the property you brought into the marriage and most of the property acquired during the marriage. Over a period of time, when separate property is commingled with marital property, it tends to lose its separate character and status (as in the house scenario above). This isn't automatic and it doesn't happen all of the time, but it's important to consider. Let's say, for example, you put inheritance money into a joint account for a short period of time because it's convenient. If you don't use that money, you can argue that its separate character is still intact. Once you have identified and classified your marital and separate assets, the next step on the road to equitably distributing the estate will be to determine all of your household's income sources and debts.

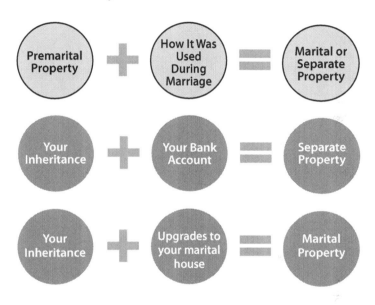

A Special Thanks to Victor G. Grossman, Attorney at Law, for his invaluable assistance with this chapter.

Income & Debt

Although electronic banking has made it harder to hide money, people still find new and inventive ways to do it. The possibility of concealed funds isn't only an issue for those married to someone who is self-employed; sometimes, the spouse who has been making money will hide it or manipulate the paperwork in such a way that some of it remains undisclosed. If you are naïve to any of this during your divorce, you are at risk of being exploited. We're not saying this to get you anxious, but forewarned is forearmed. Money makes people do strange and unpredictable things.

A lifestyle analysis is the best way to start addressing the issue. If a person claims a certain income but is living above those means—with new cars and exotic vacations, for example—there may be something going on. If you are the spouse who suspects this kind of subversive activity, know that it's sometimes hard to trace, and you may not have the resources to investigate. If you can afford it, there are forensic accountants and private detectives who can help. However, by conducting a thorough review of tax returns and credit card bills, and by knowing what to look for, you can often figure out whether there is any hanky-panky going on.

If they're not business-related, most debts will be jointly owed. Perhaps you bought a house or car or remodeled your kitchen together, or took out a second mortgage on the house to pay for the kids' college education. But what if one partner spends wildly and without the real approval of the other? It's possible that this debt will be considered the spender's. It gets complicated, so we want to reinforce how valuable counsel can be.

Once you have a good sense of your household's assets and debts, you can move forward. You can start thinking about how you would, ideally, like to see joint property distributed. All this information is also essential to determining alimony (known as spousal maintenance) and child support.

Creating Two Households

Splitting a household tends to be messy, both emotionally and financially. Often, you have two incomes supporting one cohesive unit, so how do you make it work when that unit divides? Begin to think about your financial plan for the 18–24 months following divorce. Professionals advising you should be able to help. You'll want to consider your monthly budget and what you need, realistically, to get and stay on your feet. This is where maintenance (aka alimony) and child support come into play.

Did You Know?

Alimony is an older term now generally referred to as "maintenance." It is a form of support for a former spouse. Many courts focus on maintenance for rehabilitative purposes; for example, support given to a former spouse in order for him/her to have time and training to acquire skills necessary to re-enter the workforce. Another example is support given to assist a former spouse financially if he or she is caring for young children and cannot work outside the home.

Maintenance

Most states don't have a general formula for establishing whether a spouse will receive maintenance. There also tends not to be a formula for determining how much it will be for or for how long it will be given. Judges take into account a number of factors in order to come up with the right number. These include the length of the marriage, the size of the marital estate, the lifestyle the couple is used to living, and the amount of time needed for the spouse to get back on his or her feet financially.

While the length of your marriage will affect the amount awarded either to you or your spouse, it's often the *need* for maintenance that plays a larger role. It's about what you or your ex requires in order to support an individual household. Also, as we mentioned earlier, the fact that you were abandoned or betrayed will not weigh heavily on the judge's decision. He or she will be more concerned about your ability to move on than about the circumstances that brought you to this place. Let's look at some examples:

First, there's Sue. She has been married to her husband for two and a half years, and they have two children. They both work and earn around the same amount. Does Sue need maintenance? Probably not. She and her spouse are in a similar position when it comes to establishing themselves individually.

Now, let's talk about Sam. Sam has been a stay-at-home dad for the past ten years. He is the kids' primary caretaker and has been out of the workforce for quite some time. At this point, whatever employment-related skills he had are probably rusty, and he may not be familiar with the new technology he needs to know in order to be successful. Sam needs some degree of maintenance for a period of time until he is able to re-enter the workforce and generate an income that will allow him to provide for himself and the kids.

And what about Sadie? She is middle-aged and has been married for 25 years. During this period, she held a series of part-time jobs, but nothing long-term or skill building. At this point, Sadie is used to a standard of living that, to some degree, she is entitled to continue. Her level of work experience, however, might make reaching that standard problematic, so she may be entitled to a longer term of maintenance.

When it comes to maintenance, the marital estate will also be considered. If its assets are worth $25 million and they are equitably divided, it is unlikely that either party will be able to claim a need for this provision.

Child Support

When the state determines child support, the length of the marriage does not play as big a role in the decision as it does in determining spousal maintenance. Most states, if not all, have formulas for computing child support based upon the income and assets of the parents, the number of kids, and required expenses, but in many cases there is room for adjustment. We'll use New York's formula as an example, but you should inquire about the rules in your state. The first step in New York's basic child support computation is to subtract Social Security and Medicare taxes from each parent's income up to $130,000. There may be a further reduction for city tax, but this tends to be a relatively small number. Once these deductions are made, the combined parental income is computed and then multiplied by a factor that is based on the number of children (17 percent for one child and 25 percent for two children, for example). This annual child-support amount is then allocated between the parents and is based on how much each earns. The court has discretion in applying the child support formula to income above $130,000, but many judges do so.

In many states, additional expenses are called "add-ons," and each parent must contribute. For example, childcare is often considered an add-on if the custodial parent needs to work while the children are at home. The same holds true for any particular educational, emotional, or physical need a child may have that results in additional expenses. For eample, braces tend to be considered an add-on as do activities like violin lessons for a child who is an accomplished violinist.

In most states, the amount of time each parent spends with her children affects child support. This is important, and you should ask professionals who know the local laws and judges where you live about the rules that apply to your case. There are some instances where the courts—although hesitant to move in this direction generally—will try to equalize the parents' income if the children split their time equally between both homes. For example, if the mother earns twice as much as the father she may have to provide him with funds.

As you can see, child support and custody are linked, and with custody being one of the most expensive and contentious areas of divorce litigation, getting the support you want may be more difficult than the equation lets on.

There are some parents who will be motivated to demand custody because the courts tend to give more money to the parent who spends more time with the kids. It's cynical, but it happens. Then there is also the chance that you may really believe that your ex can't do the job of raising your kids. After all your children have been through, that last thing you want is to place them in a home with a neglectful or abusive parent. At the same time, your ex may feel the same way about you.

Custody litigation can go on for years, and it's unfortunate because the very process that is meant to protect your children can hurt them in the end. If you do have an ex that is seriously disturbed, do what you have to do, but check your emotions carefully to ensure that your actions are based in reality.

You might be interested to know that most states allow parents to opt out of their respective statutory formulas if the parties can reach an agreement on how to allocate funds. The primary requirement is that the needs of the children be met.

Taxes and Divorce

Hopefully, at this point, you can see why it's so important to have a full picture of your marital estate. Without it, property cannot be fairly distributed, nor can maintenance or child support be fairly allocated. And all of these have tax implications.

Child support is neither taxable nor deductible, but maintenance is usually deductible to the person who pays it and taxable to the recipient who declares it as income. While it's not always possible to remedy this difference, emotionally healthy couples try to allocate funds so that no one is hurt financially.

For example, if your ex-spouse pays you the same amount in maintenance as your monthly mortgage payment (deductible by your ex-partner and declarable by you), and you, in turn, use that money to pay for the mortgage (deductible by you), then you come out even.

In another example, a father who is paying child support may be granted (either by agreement between the parties or by the judge) an exemption for one of his children. Generally, the tax code gives the exemption to the person with whom the child resides a majority of the time, and it's something couples tend to fight over.

Long-term Financial Goals

Whenever you are experiencing a major life change, you should consider your long-term fiscal plan. If you can afford it, meet with a financial planner. These professionals will review your finances and, based on your circumstances and future goals, will develop a plan to meet a realistic vision.

Short-term and long-term needs vary by age and stage of life. When it comes to raising kids, generating income, and meeting obligations, a 28-year-old mom with two kids is going to have different needs from a 50-year-old mom whose children are grown. The latter will probably want to focus on structuring a nest egg for her retirement years.

Getting a financial planner doesn't mean visiting your family accountant. While they may be good accountants, their focus is often too narrow. However, there are a number of accountants who are involving themselves more and more with financial planning and investment. You may want to ask your accountant if there is a financial planner that he or she recommends. Ultimately, it's up to you to choose a person with whom you are comfortable working.

Unfortunately, most attorneys are not completely equipped to help you in this area. They can give you general information and ask you to consider certain scenarios, like how you want to provide for your kids when they stay with you on weekends or how you plan to contribute to their higher education. They can also get you to start thinking, for example, about what you're going to do with the money you get from selling the house or a family car. That said, a financial professional is often in a better position to give you concrete financial advice.

A Financial Glossary

Bond: An entity's (government or corporate) promise to pay you based on the money you invest with them. The money will be repaid at a specific rate over a certain period of time.

Deferred Compensation: Includes pensions, retirement plans, 401k plans, and anything that might be received or earned that will not be paid out until later. These are long-term investments that will accrue gains and losses for both parties if they were earned during the marriage and are considered marital assets.

Disability: Defined either by the Social Security Administration or by an insurance company. Generally, it is a condition that prevents a person from functioning normally in daily life.

Equity: Broad term that includes stocks and other investments.

Gifts: Items given to you remain your property unless they are commingled with the marital estate. A piece of jewelry given to you will probably remain yours. A television you received as a wedding present will probably be considered marital.

Health insurance: If your family is supported by two incomes and you are both eligible for insurance, you will want to agree about whose policy the children will join and what the contingency plan will be if that parent loses his or her job. When deciding between the two plans consider what each costs and covers. It's trickier if one spouse and the children are insured under the other spouse's plan. In New York, once the divorce is granted, the non-employee spouse won't usually be covered, so be sure you plan according to your state's laws.

Inheritance: Money that passes from one estate to another remains wholly yours unless you comingle it with marital property. Whether it is considered a separate or marital asset will be determined by conduct: How was the money deposited or used? If, for example, you used the inheritance to upgrade your house acquired through marriage, it will be considered marital. The judge, however, may still give you credit in one way or another for the contribution you made.

Life insurance: A policy that an individual can acquire herself or through her employment that provides an amount of coverage in the event of her death. Life insurance policies are based on monthly or annual premiums and provide security for long-term obligations. They are useful in divorce because people can anticipate the financial support they will need to provide their ex-spouse and/or children. Let's say you have two young kids and know that you will be receiving child support from your ex-husband for the next 15 years, totaling $300,000.00. If you're worried about something happening to your ex, you can try to arrange that he carries at least that much in life insurance coverage that can go toward raising the kids.

Loans: If you want to claim that something was a loan rather than a gift there should be evidence for this at the time the transfer is made. If there is an expectation of repayment, it sounds like a loan. If not, it can probably be construed as a gift. When it comes to loans, it's good to have written notes.

Mortgage: A loan that must be repaid and that is secured by a piece of property.

Mutual fund: A collection of stocks, bonds, or both. It tends to be a relatively safe investment, but some mutual funds have higher risk factors or rewards than others. A financial planner can help you determine what's right for you.

Stocks: Investment vehicles that indicate partial ownership of a company. They can be held individually, jointly, or in trust. Stocks are assets that may or may not be marital depending on when and how they were acquired and by whom.

If you have any questions about how these matters may apply in your case, ask a financial expert or tax professional.

Notes

This space is for you—to remember what's important, to doodle, to make plans …

CHAPTER 10

Life after Divorce

Your State
A-Okay

There is Life
After Divorce

255

Taking Control of Your Fate

An intelligent divorce means learning all that you can about the process and its effect on you and your family so that you can join all of those who have come through it in good shape.

Certain medical and psychological problems occur more frequently in individuals who have experienced divorce or separation. It's no secret that the facts are not pretty, but it's encouraging to know that you and your children need not fall victim to these statistics. In fact, keeping in mind everything you have read so far in this book, you have quite a capable toolkit at your disposal for dealing with the risks. That being said, let's examine the following reports.

Divorced and separated mothers are more likely than mothers who are married to have a number of psychological problems. These include depression, dysthymia, Generalized Anxiety Disorder, Post-Traumatic Stress Disorder, and Antisocial Personality Disorder. They are also more likely to abuse drugs and alcohol (Afifi, Cox, and Enns, 2006).

After following a group of divorced women for ten years, researchers found that regardless of age, education, family income, change in marital status (remarriage) over the course of the study, chronic depressive symptoms, and prior illness, those who were divorced were significantly more likely to report physical illness at the ten-year mark. Illnesses ranged from colds to heart conditions and cancer (Lorenz, Wickrama, Conger, and Elder, 2006).

Compared to women, men who are in the process of separating or obtaining a divorce are more likely to have an onset of Major Depression (Bruce and Kim, 1992). Divorced men were also more than twice as likely as married men to take their own lives (Kposowa, 2000).

Back in 1970, the National Center for Health Statistics published some scary data on the link between car accidents and marital status. They found that the fatality rate was higher for divorced men and women than for those widowed, married, or single. In fact, on average, the death rate was 2.5 times higher for divorced individuals than for married individuals. Perhaps with the advent of seat belts those numbers have dropped. But since you can't legislate common sense, we recommend that you focus on driving when you're behind the wheel and leave any divorce issues you may have until you're safely in a parked position with the ignition turned off.

All of this sounds daunting, if not downright disturbing. But you have a choice.

Men, Women, and Divorce

In case you've been living in an alternate universe, you've probably noticed that fathers and mothers often deal with life a bit differently. That's because genetically, culturally, and developmentally, men and women differ from each other. From a genetic point of view, women have two X chromosomes while men have only one. Men have one Y chromosome while women have none. The male brain is bombarded by testosterone in ways that the female brain (thankfully) isn't, and the female brain deals with spikes of progesterone and estrogen in ways that men will just never fully grasp. These are real, biological differences, and they have consequences.

Now, let's consider our social environment. In most places in the world, even in the twenty-first century, men are encouraged to take aggressive roles while women are often expected to maintain family and communal roles, a pattern that probably dates back to prehistoric times.

Back then, men embarked on dangerous journeys to secure food. Killing a woolly mammoth was difficult and life-threatening. It required high energy and teamwork. Men had to be aggressive, goal-oriented, and skillful. Women stayed home in the cave and multitasked. They tended to the fire, watched the kids, kept things clean, prepared the food, tanned the skins, and sewed the garments. When her man returned, she and her children had food to eat; and she in turn would give him sex and comfort.

We can still see traces of this history in the roles men and women assume today. It's common for males to concern themselves with sports, money, and attaining power, and while women do run corporations and countries, and while there are matrilineal societies, they are few and far between.

Traditionally, the mother nurtures and grounds the family; she provides stability, but because the boy has the need to become a little man—to gain a sense of independence and foster camaraderie with other young men—he cuts ties with his family's nurturing force and risks incurring a wound deep in his soul. He'll do almost anything not to be a "mama's boy."

Being vulnerable is now frightening—to whom can he turn and still maintain his self-respect? I believe this is the core reason why so many men have difficulty being dependent. It's more than the way in which they are socialized—it seems to be inherent in their very development.

How many guys fail to ask for directions when they get lost? How many guys won't allow themselves to be "touchy-feely," even though there are times when it's appropriate? How many abusers strike their women when, in a moment of hurt and anger, she withdraws her love? It's not all about the abuser's temperament and uncontrollable rage; males find it difficult to tolerate abandonment by a person who gives them love. It strikes too close to the early wound all men endure upon leaving the nest.

Most women on the other hand, don't have to cut ties with their mothers in order to assert their own independence. That's one reason why women find comfort in community settings. It's also why they can have boundary problems and don't know when to let go. Consider all the women who have complicated relationships with their moms, yet they can't bring themselves to leave their rotten husbands and stand on their own.

Most women aren't afraid to be dependent. When they need a doctor, they go. When they are hurting, they turn to people with whom they are close. But how many men willingly visit their physicians or cry on someone else's shoulder?

Gender Specifics

Given the biological, cultural, and developmental disparities described above, it should come as no surprise that men and women handle divorce differently. Overlaps do exist, but take note of whether a gender-specific plan will work for you.

Research suggests that, when it comes to divorce, men tend to grieve later than women and to focus on their anger first (Baum, 2004). They also preoccupy themselves with the loss of their children and their family life, both of which signal a profound change in their identity (Baum, 2003; Baum, 2004).

And because male self-esteem is often deeply invested in their bank account, money becomes a primary issue. A man is not only losing his marriage; he may also be losing what he has built over time—and this can hurt a lot.

When it comes to getting the help they need, men face an obstacle. They have difficulty dealing with dependency and have a hard time counting on people. They'll avoid the doctor and won't pick up the phone to call their buddies; instead, they are likely to self-medicate with drugs and alcohol (Baum, 2003; Baum, 2004).

Unlike men, women tend to start their grieving earlier and to experience the loss of a relationship that once flourished (Baum, 2003). There is also a propensity for them to become preoccupied with their children at the expense of everything else. Luckily, women are open to relationships and to receiving support, so they are more likely than men to rely on their friends or to visit the doctor if they need help.

The action plans you are about to read aim to differentiate between the needs of men and women. That being said, each of the seven bits of advice—one for each day of the week—can be true to either gender and applied to anyone's situation.

An Action Plan for Men

1. **Reach out and don't isolate.**
   Most men prefer handling things on their own but dealing with grief requires a community. You can't do it all by yourself. Find people that understand your situation. Some of your old friends may feel awkward around you. Some couples that want to avoid taking sides won't make plans with you. That's okay. There are other people out there, both live and online. It's not bad at all to go out with other guys and let loose a little. It's okay to joke around and get some feelings off your chest. Find a support group and vent! Just don't be alone. You'll get sick.

2. **Speaking of getting sick—please see a doctor.**
   Make sure your blood pressure is okay, that you're not gaining too much weight, and that you're exercising regularly. Stress can lead to unhappy habits, like smoking, drinking, and aggressive driving. Fitness often yields good sleep and that's a key to your good health.

3. **Be careful about self-medicating.**
   Whether you like it or not, you will stress, you will grieve, and you will regress. Indulging your frustration may provide temporary relief, but it comes at a high price. M-m-m-moderation!

4. **Mind your anger.**

   Men (and many women) are prone to externalize, blaming everyone else for some of the things they do. It's important that you express your anger constructively. A good therapist may help. Too much anger at the wrong time can hurt your children or discredit you. Anger turned on yourself out of guilt and self-contempt can lead to depression, or worse.

5. **Enjoy dating.**

   This may be a nice way for you to reestablish your sense of well-being, but don't lose sight of your children; they need you now. While you may be excited about a new friend, your kids may not be initially thrilled by the idea. If you're dating, and having fun, keep it private; you don't want to confuse your kids.

6. **Get good legal help.**

   Know the laws in your state and how you're protected. All of your money will *not* go to her. But also know that the divorce is going to cost you. That's just the way it is.

7. **Be optimistic about the future.**

   You're going to get past this. You'll enjoy your children and you'll have money (though not all of it). As long as you have your health, there are new relationships on the horizon.

An Action Plan for Women

1. **You have to grieve the loss of your relationship.**
    So do it. Surround yourself with good friends; speak to your minister, priest, or rabbi; and see a therapist—whatever works. Remember that you're not going to get through this alone, and that grieving is ultimately about letting go.

2. **As for your kids: they deserve your attention.**
    That's what *The Intelligent Divorce* is all about. But kids do not benefit from an unhappy parent, so you also have to focus on taking care of yourself. Exercise, rest, eat well, and do things that make you relaxed and happy. If your children see you always preoccupied with them, you'll make them anxious.

3. **Be cautious about forming bad habits around your anger, anxiety, depression, or grief.**
    Pay attention to whether you're smoking again, drinking, doing drugs, or eating too much or too little. Get help as soon as you notice a problem. Be the grown-up!

4. **Make sure your boundaries are firm when you deal with your ex-husband and your children.**
    Be open to him, but from a position of strength. With your kids, be the adult of the house.

5. **When you're ready, it's not a bad idea to start dating.**
   It will give you a sense of the future and a feeling of confidence. Like we recommend with men, keep new relationships private. Your children don't need to be confused or fell any sense of unnecessary competition.

6. **When it comes to finances, you should consult with an attorney and inquire about your rights.**
   You will be the beneficiary of money that was part of the marriage, and maybe more depending on whether or not either of you are working. When the divorce is final, neither of you should be wiped out, but both of you will probably have less than you want.

7. **Focus on a good future for yourself and your children.**
   Let them know that you are optimistic, and do your best every single day to be exactly that. Your kids will take your lead.

A Personal Progress Chart

The charts on the following pages (feel free to copy them) will provide a chance for you to assess your behavior in relation to how you have been managing your divorce since it was first initiated. But before you even start, you must agree to be honest with yourself! Otherwise, what's the point?

This private journal is designed to help you monitor how you are doing—from assessing the grieving process, to health and fitness, to taking care of your children.

Everything you have read in this book can help you in evaluating how you are doing at this point in your life. As you periodically document your progress, you may discover that you need some help. That's perfectly natural. Divorce can present psychological and physical hazards, but you can increase the likelihood of coming through it okay when you are honest with yourself and take clear steps to fix the things that can be fixed.

If you are consistently showing signs of stress related problems, please consult your doctor, who can test you for any medical issues and refer you to the appropriate specialist for the specific help you may need.

Keep positive. You can get through this.

How Am I Doing?							
0 – Does Not Exhibit the Behavior 1 – Infrequently 2 – Sometimes 3 – Frequently **Symptoms**	Time after divorce has been announced						
	Before Divorce	Immediately after	One Week	One Month	Three Months	Six Months	One Year
Stages of Grief							
Denial							
Anger							
Bargaining							
Depression							
Acceptance							
Emotional Problems							
I am overly anxious							
I have panic attacks							
I feel depressed							
I am overly euphoric							
I have suicidal thoughts							
I am too tearful							
I always feel guilty							
I am easily fatigued							
I quickly lose my temper							
I am impatient							
I have racing thoughts							
I am too suspicious							
I am lonely							

How Am I Doing?							
0 – Does Not Exhibit the Behavior 1 – Infrequently 2 – Sometimes 3 – Frequently Symptoms	Time after divorce has been announced						
	Before Divorce	Immediately after	One Week	One Month	Three Months	Six Months	One Year
Behavioral Problems							
I have no appetite							
I eat too much							
I am easily distracted							
I struggle with addiction(s)							
I struggle with my memory							
I lie regularly							
I am stalking my ex							
I am never home							
Problems at Work							
I am poorly organized							
I am frequently absent							
I am criticized by my boss							
I avoid challenges							
Socialization							
I do not see friends							
I would rather stay home							
I feel lonely/isolated							
I have unhealthy sexual behavior							
I am dating erratically							

How Am I Doing?

0 – Does Not Exhibit the Behavior 1 – Infrequently 2 – Sometimes 3 – Frequently Symptoms	Time after divorce has been announced						
	Before Divorce	Immediately after	One Week	One Month	Three Months	Six Months	One Year
Parenting							
I often break the Intergenerational Boundary							
I use my kids as messengers							
I need my kids for support							
I bad mouth my ex to my kids							
I am inconsistent with enforcing rules							
I yell too much							
I am too passive as a parent							
I am too controlling							
I buy the kids too much stuff							
I can't sleep alone							
I am into myself and not into them							

This set of questions is positive in nature. Hopefully, you have learned from various chapters in this book to recognize your own shortcomings and are now taking clear and thoughtful steps to find solutions and forge a new path for yourself and your children. That being said, your job is not over. It's vital to affirm your progress, to announce it proudly to yourself, and to take ownership of your life.

How Am I Doing?							
0 – Does Not Exhibit the Behavior	Time after divorce has been announced						
1 – Infrequently 2 – Sometimes 3 – Frequently **Symptoms**	Before Divorce	Immediately after	One Week	One Month	Three Months	Six Months	One Year
Health (mind, body and spirit)							
I maintain an exercise routine							
I am maintaining a nutritional diet							
I am finding a supportive community							
I regularly reach out to friends							
I find pleasure in dating							
I enjoy a spiritual path (whatever that is for you)							
I am on top of my finances							
I am regularly optimistic							
I feel fulfilled as a parent							
I am a good role model							

SCRAPBOOK
WHAT DIVORCE HAS TAUGHT ME ABOUT MYSELF

Right away, I learned the importance of fighting and not sweeping things under the rug. In my second marriage, we have had quite a lot more fighting and making up. My view of marriage now is that it is a spiritual practice—a path to growth and hopefully to wisdom—and certainly not a source of happiness in itself.

I am far from perfect and there is no perfect way to go through this process. I have learned to let go and trust the precious bond I have with my child, even when we are not physically together. I have learned to ignore other people's ideas about how I "should" or "shouldn't" be in the context of our nontraditional family situation.

I was afraid every step of the way. So I broke down my divorce into steps and that gave me courage.

I am stronger, more independent, and more capable than I ever gave myself credit for.

I have learned how to react less and respond more. I have learned how important it is to yield to the other parent's wishes whenever possible in order to preserve a working relationship for the bene t of our son.

My divorce was absolutely essential to the process of freeing and healing myself.

Notes

This space is for you—to remember what's important, to doodle, to make plans …

Conclusion

Looking at Yourself with Pride

My practice is comprised of children, adolescents, and adults. Typically, they are suffering from something, whether it's bulimia, addiction, poor academics, or divorce. After an initial session or two, I tend to do something that catches their attention.

While they're sitting on the couch, I get up, open the door, and say to them, "I'm inviting your future self into the room." I then close the door, look back at my patient, and say, "Let's take a look at your future self." I motion this imaginary person to a chair, as if she is sitting down with us.

I tell my patient that her future self wants her to be proud of the work she does in my office. I may not be there for them ten years from now, but her future certainly will be. I turn to the imaginary figure and say "whatever your younger self and I do together has an impact on you. I want you to be happy with what we have done."

Most patients laugh or smile wryly. But everybody gets it. It's not about a power struggle or about improving in black-and-white terms. It's about being productive and actually impacting that future self.

Some patients will say, "You know, Dr. Banschick, I don't have an image of a future self." Giving them the chance to consider what they may be like in ten years can be useful. It reminds them that something important is really at stake. And for many, this exercise rings true.

So here we are at the end of this book. Your future self should look back on this period in your life with pride. All of the work you have engaged in—grieving the loss of your marriage and the family structure you once had, taking charge of your anger and your anxiety, and striving to collaborate with your ex-spouse—are all predicated on the notion that when you take good care of yourself you will have the strength and stability to handle things wisely.

We have given you a whole set of tools. You don't have to implement every one. Some won't apply. But if you take care of your body, mind, and soul, you'll be surprised by how much power you have. Once you have some real power, you can change yourself and deal properly with the people in your life.

With your ex, strive for perspective, good limits, and a collaborative relationship. Achieving these things takes work, but remember that you have people available to help you when you need it, like friends, family, therapists, attorneys, and, in more serious cases, law-enforcement officials. Use the tools at your disposal wisely, for when your judgment is clouded and you operate out of hate you only make things harder for your children and your own future.

When it comes to your kids, know that modeling is everything. They need to see that you are on top of your game. That doesn't mean that you're perfect. That means that you're grieving properly, getting the support you need, and are aware of what you're going through. This moment in your life won't last forever; there will be an end.

Your children need to see that you're stable and trying your best. Protect the Intergenerational Boundary. You're the parent, and your kids must remain kids. When you set positive examples for your children, you defeat the repetition compulsion and the scripts that were written for you when you were young. When you give your children something better than you had, you repair the past and make the future a better place.

I believe that creating a healthy childhood for our kids is one of the greatest gifts each of us can provide to the world. This is particularly trying in divorce, but it is possible, and I've seen it happen.

I wish you good luck through the hard work this takes.

Have confidence that you're capable of great things.

A Practical Approach for Parents

Let's turn theory into action. Everything you know about what's right for you and your kids—and all the tools you've learned in this book—won't mean anything unless you use them effectively with your children and at least attempt to deal constructively with your ex.

Here are two moral agreements between parents, providing an honorable way for you to raise your children wisely in a spirit of collaboration. These legally nonbinding contracts are intended to act upon your legitimate wish for a constructive relationship in the midst of divorce.

It's a potential win/win for everyone in your family.

You tried you best to make a successful marriage. Now, for the sake of your children and your own self-respect, you should not tolerate a failed divorce. After all is said and done, when the lawyers are paid and the waiting and worrying is over, it's really up to you and your ex to determine how you're going to move forward into the future—together but apart—for the benefit of everyone.

This new commitment should be taken as seriously as any commitment that you have ever made. Most important, it's a benevolent agreement between the two of you as living, breathing human beings, above and beyond any court's jurisdiction.

Primary principle: no matter what, put your children first.

As for the ground rules and temperament of your agreement, it's easier to liberalize from a conservative position than to become more conservative from a liberal stance. Make the agreement formal and rigid until you see how you, your ex-spouse, and your kids are doing. You can always loosen it up later if things go smoothly.

Schedule a regular time to review how you're both doing. Strike when the iron is cold, when nothing of vital importance is happening. Your goal is to build up trust in your alliance for the sake of your kids' well-being.

You should feel proud that you've come this far. Now it's time to go a couple of steps further and give your kids something to feel proud of when they grow up.

A seven-year-old finds stability during her parents' divorce, as featured with Dr. Banschick on CBS's *The Early Show*.

An Agreement for Our Children

1. **We will put our children first.** This means that we agree not to speak badly about each other in front of our children. We agree to do everything in our power to protect their innocence.

2. **We will respect Intergenerational Boundaries.** This means that we will do everything in our power *not* to expose the children to adult problems. They need not be concerned about taking care of either of us. We will not lean on them for support. They should not have access to any of our private communications, whether on the phone or via the internet. Our children will not be used to pass messages between us.

3. **We will secure outside help to support our children whenever it's required.** This means that our children may encounter difficulties requiring special attention. This may be as a consequence of the divorce or may have come about independently. He or she may have school issues or problems in one of our homes. We agree to get professional advice when appropriate, like a learning evaluation for a child having difficulties at school or a psychological evaluation for a child who is showing emotional upset.

4. **We will expose our children to our significant others only after an appropriate delay.** This means that our children need not know about someone either of us may be dating. It takes a long time for a child to get through a divorce, and the notion of being displaced by another adult may be too much to bear. We commit ourselves to keeping our romantic relationships private until a significant time has passed, and until this relationship has become serious.

Note: This is a nonbinding parenting agreement. It is a moral contract and not a legal commitment. It is designed to keep us on track regarding the health of our children during and after our divorce.

Mother: _____ Date: _____

Father: _____ Date: _____

An Agreement Between Parents

1. **We will let go of a win-lose attitude and be willing to compromise.** This means that we need to work together for the sake of our children. The many power struggles of divorce can derail us from the hard work of collaboration. We pledge to take each problem as it comes and attempt to solve it in good faith. We understand that if we are successful in building a healthy and positive relationship into the future, it will be best for our children.

2. **We will respect each other's boundaries.** This means that we will do everything in our power not to impose ourselves unnecessarily on each other. For instance, if a conversation is getting heated, it's understood that a boundary may have been crossed, and that the conversation may be tabled temporarily. We will respect the boundaries of our respective homes and will visit or enter only upon invitation. We are not entitled to visit unannounced, nor can we expect that every time we telephone our kids they will be available to speak with us.

3. **We will create a safe way to communicate.** This means that there should never be abuse of any kind. We will make all attempts to speak with each other respectfully, with the intention of creating a safe environment for constructive communication.

4. **We will periodically review how things are going.** This means that we commit ourselves to reviewing the status of each of our children, as well as our efforts at collaboration. How is everybody doing? Is the Intergenerational Boundary more or less intact? These reviews can be weekly, monthly, or less frequent, as required by our situation.

5. **We agree to get outside help if our ability to work together breaks down.** This means that we make parenting decisions together as often as possible. If we have difficulty with an important issue—school, what to tell the kids, introducing a significant other—we agree to get some insight from a child-development professional about that specific issue.

6. **We both know that mistakes will happen.** This means that we know it's a lot of work to keep the Intergenerational Boundary intact, respect each other's boundaries, and practice the art of active listening when people are stressed. People sometimes say or do inappropriate things when under pressure. Let's agree to cut each other a bit of slack, whenever possible.

Note: This is a nonbinding parenting agreement. It is a moral contract and not a legal commitment. It is designed to keep us on track regarding the health of our children during and after our divorce.

Mother: _____ Date: _____

Father: _____ Date: _____

Your Child's Bill of Rights

1. Don't ask me to choose sides.

2. Spare me the details of your legal proceedings.

3. Don't complain to me or lean on me. It's too much.

4. Give me privacy on the phone with my other parent.

5. Don't cross-examine me afterward.

6. I am not your messenger.

7. Don't ever ask me to lie to either parent.

8. Listen to me when I have something to say.

9. No guilt trips, no matter what.

10. Don't spoil me, even if you do feel guilty.

Adapted from The New York Law Journal (1996)

Resources

Recommended Reading

Caught in the Middle—Protecting the Children of High-Conflict Divorce.

Garrity and Barris, Jossey-Bass, 1994.

Cybersex: The Dark Side of the Force. Al Cooper. Brunner-Routledge, 2000.

Divorce Poison. Richard Warshak. HarperCollins, 2003.

Divorce Wars. Jeffery Leving. Collins Press, 2007.

Full Catastrophe Living. Jon Kabat-Zinn. Delacorte Press, 1990.

Getting Up,Getting Over, and Getting On: A Twelve Step Approach to Divorce Recovery.

Micki McWade. Champion Press, 1999.

Healing Words. Larry Dossey. HarperSanFrancisco, 1993.

How to Help Your Children Overcome Your Divorce.

Elissa Benedek and Catherine Brown. New Market Press, 1998.

No-Fight Divorce. Brette McWhorter Sember. McGraw-Hill, 2005.

Second Chances. Judith Wallerstein and Sandra Blakeslee. Houghton Mifflin, 1996.

Stop Fighting Over the Kids. Mike Mastracci. St. Gabriel's Press, 2009.

Surviving the Break Up: How Children and Parents Cope with Divorce.

Judith Wallerstein and Joan Kelly. Basic Books, 1980.

Surviving Separation and Divorce: A Woman's Guide (2nd Ed.)
Lorianne Hoff Oberlin. Adams Media, 2005.

Taking Charge of ADHD. Russell A. Barkley. The Guilford Press, 2000.

The Complete Guide for Men and Women Divorcing.
Melvin Belli and Mel Krantzler. St. Martin's Griffin, 1988.

The Divorced Parent: Success Strategies for Raising Your Children after Separation.
Stephanie Marston. Pocket Books, 1994.

The Feeling Good Handbook. David Burns. William & Morrow, 1990.

The Magic Years. Selma Fraiberg. Scribner, 1956.

The Relaxation Response. Herbert Benson. William Morrow, 1975.

Vicky Lansky's Divorce Book for Parents. New American Library, 1989.

Wherever You Go There You Are. Jon Kabat-Zinn. Hyperion, 1994.

Recommended Read-Aloud Books For Children

Dinosaurs Divorce. Marc Brown and Laurie Brown. Little, Brown Young Readers, 1988.

How It Feels When Parents Divorce. Jill Krementz. Knopf, 1984

I Don't Want to Talk About It. Jeanie Franz Ransom. Magination Press, 2000.

It's Not Your Fault, Koko Bear: A Read-Together Book for Parents and Young Children During Divorce. Vicki Lansky. The Book Peddlers, 1997.

Mamma and Daddy Bears Divorce. Cornelia Maude Spelman.

Albert Whitman & Company, 1998.

Two Homes. Claire Masurel. Candlewick, 2003.

Was It the Chocolate Pudding? A Story for Little Kids About Divorce. Sandra Levins.

American Psychological Association, 2005.

What Would You Do? A Child's Book About Divorce.

Barbara Cain and Elissa Benedek. American Psychiatric Association, 1986.

When Mom and Dad Divorce. Emily Menendez-Aponte and R. W. Alley. Abbey Press, 1999.

When My Parents Forgot How to Be Friends (Let's Talk About It!).

Jennifer Moore-Mallinos. Barron's Educational Series, 2005.

Recommended Reading for Pre-teens

Divorce Happens to the Nicest Kids: A Self-Help Book.

Michael S. Prokop. Alegra House, 1996.

Divorced but Still My Parents. Shirley Thomas, Dorothy Rankin, Holliday Thompson. Springboard Publications, 1998.

How to Survive Your Parents' Divorce: A Kids' Advice to Kids.

Gayle Kimball. Equality, 1994.

My Family's Changing. (A First Look At Series). Pat Thomas.

Barron's Educational Series, 1999.

My Parents Still Love Me Even Though They're Getting Divorced.

Lois V. Nightingale. 1994

What Am I Doing in a Stepfamily? Claire Berman. Carol Publishing Group, 1992.

Why Are We Getting a Divorce? Peter Mayle. Harmony Books, 1988.

Recommended Reading for Teens

Keeping Your Life Together When Your Parents Pull Apart: A Teen's Guide to Surviving Divorce. Angela Elwell Hunt. Backinprint.Com, 2000.

Making Your Way after Your Parents' Divorce: A Supportive Guide for Personal Growth.

Lynn Casella. Liguori Publications, 2002.

Now What Do I Do? A Guide to Help Teenagers with Their Parents' Separation or Divorce. Lynn Cassella-Kapusinski. ACTA Publications, 2006.

Split: a Graphic Reality Check for Teens Dealing with Divorce. Marcus Brotherton. Multnomah Books, 2006.

Surviving Divorce: Teens Talk About What Hurts and What Helps. Trudi Strain. Trueit. Children's Press CT, March 2007.

Taking Good Care of Yourself: For Teens Going Through Separation and Divorce.

Risa J. Garon. Children of Separation and Divorce Center Inc., 1994.

The Divorce Helpbook for Teens. Cynthia MacGregor. Impact Publishers, May 2004.

Movies with Divorce Themes

For Preteens

A Perfect World (1993)

Shy son of single mother inadvertently kidnapped by unstable crook (Kevin Costner). Forced to evade Texas Ranger (Clint Eastwood), the boy and his captor form a special bond. Boy learns lessons of independence and morality.

ET (1982)

Boy takes care of an alien after his family splits up in a divorce. Spielberg's own childhood of divorce softened by an imaginary friend has been reported to be the inspiration behind this film.

Imagine That (2009)

A career-driven father (Eddie Murphy) reconnects with his daughter after separation from his wife. Realizes his daughter has special powers that can benefit his job. As he uses these powers to get ahead, he also finds himself growing closer and closer to his once estranged daughter.

Karate Kid (1984)

Angst-riddled son of a single mother has trouble dealing with bullies at school. He befriends a local karate master who becomes his mentor and teaches him discipline through the use of Karate. A 1980's cult classic.

Liar Liar (1997)

Less than honest newly divorced father (Jim Carrey) is too focused on his job. Child's birthday wish is that his father can no longer tell lies to anyone. Through this birthday wish, both son and father grow closer together.

Mrs. Doubtfire (1994)

Sally Field files for divorce from Robin Williams, gaining custody of three children. To spend more time with his children, Williams disguises himself as a female housekeeper.

The Parent Trap (1999)

Twins (both portrayed by Lindsay Lohan), separated at birth due to their parents' divorce, are reunited at summer camp. They switch places to spend time with the opposite parent and conspire to reunite their mother and father (Natasha Richardson and Dennis Quaid).

Toy Story Three (2010)

A single mother is seen raising a son who is about to separate and go off to college. In the meantime this young man has to separate from his childhood toys as well, who feel abandoned. The movie is about the fear of being left behind and the redemption that only love can bring.

For Teens

Boyz N the Hood (1992)

Explores social woes of south central Los Angeles through the eyes of several black youths, from their childhoods to their lives as adults; portrays struggle to escape environment of broken homes, drugs, and violence while striving for bigger and better things (Laurence Fishburne).

Irreconcilable Differences (1984)

Woman (Drew Barrymore) remembers the bitter divorce between her two egocentric parents. The divorce was so unbearable that the child version of the woman filed for emancipation from her parents to go live with the maid.

Life As a House (2001)

Father with terminal cancer (Kevin Kline) takes custody of his misanthropic teenage son, who is deep into drugs, small-time prostitution, and avoidance of his father.

Lost in Yonkers (1993)

When World War II breaks out, widowed man (Richard Dreyfus) must leave his two children in the eccentric hands of their grandmother and aunt. This is Neil Simon's poignant adaptation of his Broadway play.

Man of the House (1995)

Chevy Chase marries a single mother, Farah Fawcett, and hopes to gain the respect of her son from a previous marriage.

Stepmom (1999)

Julia Roberts plays the younger girlfriend of a divorced father (Ed Harris). She attempts to win over his two young children who are still very close to their biological mother, Susan Sarandon.

The Man Without a Face (1994)

Mel Gibson plays a teacher and local social pariah, due to a horrific accident 10 years earlier for which he was held responsible. He befriends a fatherless, 13-year-old boy and both help each other deal with an unwelcoming world.

The Squid and the Whale (2006)

Jeff Daniels and Laura Linney play divorcing intellectuals whose sons take sides and form new bonds with the parent they decide to live with.

For Adults

Bye Bye Love (1995)

Three male friends deal with new lives after divorce, including children, ex-wives, adult homelessness, and new girlfriends. Local radio psychologist offers his own advice for each of the three men.

Dinner with Friends (2002)

Comedy/drama about happily married couple (Dennis Quaid and Andi MacDowell). When close friends divorce after twelve years of marriage, they reexamine their own situation.

Kramer vs. Kramer (1980)

Dustin Hoffman and Meryl Streep as divorced couple, this film previews the eventual adoption of the "best interests of the child" doctrine in family law.
Oscars: Best Actor, Best Actress, Best Director, Best Screenplay, Best Picture.

Sleepless in Seattle (1994)

Tom Hanks plays a newly widowed father who moves to Seattle with his son, who calls a local self-help radio station to look for a new wife for his dad, who ends up with national attention from many women. Meg Ryan reevaluates her own relationship and ends up heading west.

War of the Roses (1990)

Kathleen Turner and Michael Douglas are seeking divorce but both want to keep the house and go to great lengths to kick the other one out of a beloved home, while divorce lawyer (Danny DeVito) is stuck in the middle.

Yoga References

Choudhury, B. (2000). *Bikram's Beginning Yoga Class.* New York: Penguin Putnam

Faulds, R. (2006). *Kripalu Yoga: A Guide to Practice ON and Off the Mat.* New York: Bantam

Lasater, J. (2000). *Living Your Yoga.* Berkley, California: Rodmell Press

Lee, C. (2004). *Yoga Body, Buddha Mind.* New York: Riverhead Books

Internet Resources

Professional Sites

American Academy of Child & Adolescent Psychiatry
(*www.aacap.org*)

American Academy of Matrimonial Lawyers (*www.aaml.org*)

American Association for Marriage and Family Therapy
(*www.aamft.org*)

American Association of Pastoral Counselors (*www.aapc.org*)

American Psychological Association *(www.apa.org)*

American Psychiatric Association *(www.psych.org)*

IACP, The International Academy of Collaborative Professionals *(www.collaborativepractice.com)*

National Association of Social Workers *(www.socialworkers.org)*

National Center for Missing and Exploited Children *(missingkids.com)*

Parenting/Network Sites

Child-Centered Divorce *(www.childcentereddivorce.com)*

Child Development *(www.childdevelopmentinfo.com)*

Divorce Support *(www.divorcesupport.com)*

Divorce Network *(www.divorcenetwork.com)*

Early Childhood Development *(www.cdc.gov/ncbddd/child/)*

First Wives World *(www.firstwivesworld.com)*

National Center for Fathering *(www.fathers.com)*

PBS Parents *(pbs.org/parents/childdevelopment)*

Self Help *(www.helpself.com/directory/divorce)*

The Divorce Portal *(www.thedivorceportal.com)*

The Intelligent Divorce *(www.theintelligentdivorce.com)*

Common Psychiatric and Personality Disorders

Adjustment Disorder (AD)

The issues that arise because of a divorce can often put a lot of stress on children. An adjustment disorder is a powerful reaction to a stressor, such as divorce. In general, patients will have substantial distress in excess of what should be expected from a certain type of stress. Due to the many ways adults and children respond to stress, numerous subtypes of adjustment disorders have been documented.

For further information on Adjustment Disorder:
www.nlm.nih.gov/medlineplus/ency/article/000932.htm

Attention Deficit Hyperactivity Disorder (ADHD)

It is estimated that 3 to 5 percent of children in the United States suffer from some degree of ADHD. Inattention, hyperactivity, and impulsivity are the hallmarks that comprise a diagnosis for ADHD, but some children (and adults) are primarily inattentive.

For further information on ADHD:
www.nimh.nih.gov/health/publications/attention-deficit-hyperactivity-disorder/complete-index.shtml

Bipolar Disorder

Children and adolescents may exude severe moodiness, switching between aggression and high-energy behaviors to frank depressive episodes. Psychiatrists are only now better realizing what this problem appears like in childhood and especially in adolescence where it has been found to be more common than once thought.

For further information on Bipolar Disorder:

www.nami.org/Template.cfm?Section=By_Illness&template=/ ContentManagement/ContentDisplay.cfm&ContentID=13107

Chemical Dependency/Abuse

Alcohol and substance abuse are all too common under the stress of divorce. Sometimes, one or both contribute to the family's breakup. It's no secret that it's hard to live with an alcoholic husband or a wife who is abusing prescription drugs.

The strain of divorce itself can cause chemical dependency and abuse. Addiction can be part and parcel of a depression, a bipolar deterioration, or a character problem, and it is always destructive to parenting, co-parenting, and life in general.

The treatment for chemical dependency and abuse is both social and psychiatric. Alcoholics Anonymous is an amazing organization that helps addicts stay committed to recovery despite the pressure to give in to their illness. Treatment for underlying psychological problems, like depression or Bipolar Disorder, is also essential. Sometimes, rehabilitative hospitalization is required to clean out the body and to determine an appropriate course of treatment. Like resetting a computer, this gives the patient an opportunity to start fresh.

For further information on Chemical Dependency/Abuse:

http://www.nicd.us/

Dysthymic Disorder

This common type of depression is low-grade and affects both children and adults; it can also sometimes progress to major depression or other mood disorders.

For further information on Dysthymic Disorder:
www.nlm.nih.gov/medlineplus/ency/article/000918.htm

Eating Disorders

There are two main types of eating disorders: anorexia and bulimia. Both are marked by destructive eating habits. Frequently, eating disorders will manifest in conjunction with another psychological disorder such as depression or anxiety disorders. These disorders predominantly occur in women; 85 to 95 percent of patients with anorexia, and 65 to 70 percent of bulimia patients who are women. In the case of young people, bulimia affects one to three of every 100 adolescents, while anorexia affects one of every 100–200 adolescent girls. Eating disorders are less common in adults.

For further information on Eating Disorders:
www.nimh.nih.gov/health/publications/eating-disorders/
complete-index.shtml

Major Depressive Disorder

This type of depression is so severe, it has the potential to undermine every facet of a person's life, whether it's a child or an adult, from academic performance to interaction with others. Studies indicate that major depressive disorder is common in adults and somewhat less so among children. This type of depression can manifest as a single or a recurring episode.

For further information on Major Depressive Disorder:
www.mentalhealth.samhsa.gov/publications/allpubs/CA-0011/ default.asp

Panic Disorder

Panic disorder is an anxiety disorder and is identified by unexpected and repeated episodes of intense fear accompanied by physical distress. These episodes are called "panic attacks" and can last anywhere from minutes to hours depending upon the degree of severity. More than 3 million Americans will suffer from panic disorder in their lifetime. In many cases, agoraphobia, the fear of outside environments or environments in which hurried escape could cause humiliation, can also accompany panic disorder.

For further information on Panic Disorder:
www.aacap.org/page.ww?name=Panic+Disorder+in+Children+ and+Adolescents&section=Facts+for+Families

Obsessive Compulsive Disorder (OCD)

Repetitive behaviors and thoughts that interfere with everyday life are classified as OCD. In the United States, it is reported that as many as one in two hundred adolescents suffer from obsessive compulsive disorder. OCD often continues into adult life.

For further information on Obsessive Compulsive Disorder:
www.aacap.org/cs/root/facts_for_families/obsessivecompulsive_ disorder_in_children_and_adolescents

Oppositional Defiant Disorder (ODD)

Although children may be insubordinate from time to time, frequent and consistent disobedience with authority figures can potentially be diagnosed as ODD. The frequency of this disorder rivals ADHD in the population.

For further information on ODD:
www.aacap.org/cs/root/facts_for_families/children_with_ oppositional_defiant_disorder

Pervasive Developmental Disorder

Disorders classified as Pervasive Developmental Disorders are disorders that deal with irregularities in social and communication skills in individuals. These include diagnoses such as autism and Asperger's syndrome. The average onset of such disorders is approximately three years of age; however, parents may observe irregular behavior as early as infancy.

For further information on Pervasive Developmental Disorder:
www.ninds.nih.gov/disorders/pdd/pdd.htm

Post-Traumatic Stress Disorder (PTSD)

Post-Traumatic Stress Disorder is not limited to persons who witness, or who are involved in combat, but since the start of the Iraq and Afghanistan wars, the public has become more aware of the diagnosis. PTSD is characterized by long-lasting fear and anxiety, typically resulting from severe stress and trauma. People with this disorder are hypervigilant and experience startle reactions, intrusive dreams, and recurrent disturbing memories, called flashbacks. PTSD can be truly disabling, causing its sufferers fright at every turn.

Let's look at how PTSD might develop. Consider a soldier who, in the midst of battle, sees her friend die. Upon return to civilian life, she is highly reactive, psychologically revisiting the moment of injury whenever a door slams or when a car alarm goes off. It's as if the trauma lives inside of her, waiting to be triggered, and when it is, it's like she's back at the scene.

PTSD affects rape victims, victims of violence, and even those who have experienced verbal abuse. We aren't certain about why some get the disorder and others don't, but if you have it—no matter the source of trauma—your divorce may well expose your pain. If you're suffering from PTSD, seek help; it's best for you and for your family. Treatments are excellent, and they include supportive psychotherapy and medication.

For further information on Post-Traumatic Stress Disorder (PTSD):
www.nimh.nih.gov/health/topics/post-traumatic-stress-disorder-ptsd/index.shtml

Psychotic Disorders

Individuals with psychotic disorders have abnormal perceptions and thoughts. They have an altered sense of reality and will often suffer from delusions or hallucinations. Delusions occur when an individual with a psychotic disorder will believe inaccurate information even when presented with the truth; hallucinations deal with the sensory facet of the individual. People who suffer from hallucinations will often hear or see things that are not present.

For further information on Psychotic Disorders:
www.nlm.nih.gov/medlineplus/psychoticdisorders.html

Reactive Attachment Disorder (in young children)

This unfortunate mental disorder occurs when young children do not form a healthy bond with their caregivers. Usually, Reactive Attachment Disorder takes place in abusive environments or environments of neglect. It can sometimes be found in adopted children.

For further information on Reactive Attachment Disorder:
www.aacap.org/cs/root/facts_for_families/reactive_attachment_ disorder

Separation Anxiety Disorder

Parents are usually the primary caregivers for their children, creating a powerful attachment bond. Within a divorce, a prolonged or abrupt separation from a caring adult can cause stress and the child may respond in the form of separation anxiety disorder. Statistically, one in twenty-five children have separation anxiety disorder. This disorder manifests once a specific person leaves the presence of the child.

For further information on Separation Anxiety Disorder:
www.mentalhealth.samhsa.gov/publications/allpubs/CA-0007/ dafault.asp

Common Personality Problems

Personality disorders are characterized by a long-standing set of patterns and behaviors an individual may exhibit. There are a number of these disorders, and by definition they are dysfunctional.

Most personality-disordered individuals are unhappy, and they make others unhappy, too. For some, the experience of the disorder is internal, characterized by chronic upset, suicidal thoughts, paranoia, or dependency. For others, it's external, and they make people around them feel criticized, judged, used, or manipulated.

Most people with personality disorders are not interested in treatment because they see their problems as outside of themselves. This is very sad. It's common for someone like this to tell her therapist that, "If I only my ex were a better person then everything would be okay."

Often, there is a kernel of truth in their narrative, but when the therapist takes a full history and hears the rest of her story, it becomes clear that something isn't right—that the person sitting on the couch is stuck and has been so for a long time.

If you're developing this disorder, or if you're divorcing someone who has it, then it's likely that your life is now very difficult.

You'll note the similarity between some of the personality disorders included in this chapter and the character traps we've talked about throughout the book. The key is that a person with a Personality Disorder—a formal diagnosis—probably had it for years before the divorce and will continue to have it once you've both moved on. Character traps, on the other hand, are a heuristic device developed to help you manage an ex-spouse who, due to stress, has dropped into a temporary state of problematic thinking and behaving. While they look very much like personality disorders (and while our tips for managing them can be similarly applied) the good news is that, once the strain of divorce has lifted, people suffering from character traps tend to bounce back to their normal selves.

Antisocial Personality Disorder

In some ways, this is the most serious social disease found in psychiatry. Often, people with an Antisocial Personality Disorder have a history of abusing animals when young and of lighting fires, among other cruel and dangerous activities. As kids, they tend to carry the diagnosis of Oppositional Defiant Disorder, and as teens, of Conduct Disorder.

Individuals with Antisocial Personality Disorder display an ongoing pattern of exploitation, often engage in criminal activity, and have no sense of right and wrong. If you're divorcing someone with this problem, it's crucial that you set and enforce good limits. The jail system is filled with Antisocials, but there are a number of them who are smart and capable enough to appear healthy while living a secret life of manipulation and destruction.

Borderline Personality Disorder:

These patients usually have a teenage history of serious mood instability and acting out. Binging, purging, drug and alcohol abuse, and indiscriminate sex are among the highly stimulating ways they keep themselves from feeling empty. The Borderline suffers from a chronic void and is often desperately depressed. If a person with this disorder survives into her thirties, the good news is that she often gets better on her own. Once the sturm und drang of youth has passed, brain development allows for more mature engagement with the world.

Patients with Borderline Personality Disorder are often in therapy and are among the most difficult to treat. They tend to lie and manipulate, and they are so intent on seeking relief from their ennui that they can't do the work of a disciplined adult. People close to them are often held hostage to their moods and may assume the duty of protecting them from themselves. Borderlines sometimes pose disturbing threats to their physical safety.

Dependent Personality Disorder

This personality disorder is characterized by a severe and comprehensive lack of confidence. She never feels comfortable making decisions, believes she can't make it on her own, is always seeking help, and is preoccupied with self-pity. The Dependent Personality Disorder has much in common with the Victim character trap, but it's longer lasting and more deeply buried.

Often, patients with this diagnosis experienced severe trauma in their early life and never developed a basic sense of trust in their own capacities. As a result, they can lean too much on their kids or their lawyers and are sometimes vulnerable to exploitation by their ex-husband or wife (especially when he or she is an Antisocial or a Narcissist).

Treatment can be effective, but people with dependency issues must confront the requirement to grow up, individuate, and become their own person. This means tolerating the anxiety of making wrong decisions and living with them. These individuals are vulnerable to depressive disorders, chemical dependency, and abuse.

Narcissistic Personality Disorder

This personality disorder is similar to the Narcissist character trap, but it precedes the divorce and will be around well after it's over. Narcissists see everyone as an object to be used for their gratification. They are often preoccupied with what others think of them and usually are endowed with some great asset, like good looks, talent, charisma, wealth, or fame. Often, Narcissists use these qualities to avoid accountability—people simply forgive them, even though, despite their protests to the contrary, they simply don't care.

Narcissists care first, and only, about themselves. They can't help it, and they rarely have the self-reflection to see their shallowness. This is because they are so preoccupied with their image that they game themselves into thinking they are better people than they really are. If you're a Narcissist, treatment will be difficult. It will push you to realize that you're not special, and that's painful. The paradox, however, is that by realizing your own conventionality you actually become special. Stick it out in therapy and know that, as you mature, your relationships will improve and you may find some peace.

If you're divorcing a Narcissist, much like the Antisocial, it's recommended that you keep perspective, maintain boundaries, and set good limits. Know that the Narcissist will always think that you are wrong and they are right, and they will disappoint you time and again. Many have an "out of sight, out of mind" mentality—even with their kids.

Paranoid Personality Disorder

A person with this disorder is fundamentally untrusting. They rarely enter treatment, but they are regularly seen in court. They can easily play the Victim role, and they obviously mirror the Paranoid character trap. When under extreme stress, these unfortunate people can suffer from paranoid delusions.

The Intelligent Consumer:
A Guide to Psychiatric Medicine

The Food and Drug Administration (FDA) approves medicines for use with adults, teens, and children. It approves drugs for specific indications, but the government allows doctors some leeway to use medicine for "off-label" (not yet approved) care. Ask your doctor whether the medicine being prescribed for you or your child is for an FDA-approved condition. If he or she is prescribing off-label, ask for his or her rationale and experience with this approach, since it is not yet government approved.

Information about side effects can be found at the American Academy of Child and Adolescent Psychiatry website (www.aacap.org) as well as the FDA website (www.fda.gov). For more complete information, ask your doctor.

Here are some of the more common categories of medication prescribed for adults, teens, and children who may be experiencing unusually stressful situations, even temporarily, such as divorce.

Stimulants

This class of pharmaceuticals includes some of the most commonly prescribed medications in child and adolescent psychiatry, which are also increasingly being used among adults. Stimulants have been studied thoroughly over the past 30 years and have proven effective in the treatment of Attention Deficit

Disorder and related problems. As with other medications, this class of drugs has its own set of side effects to consider. Consult your prescribing doctor to discuss your options.

Anxiolytics

Anti-anxiety drugs are very useful for short-term reduction of anxiety. They work quickly and effectively but there is some potential for abuse. They need to be monitored carefully. Disorders such as Separation Anxiety, OCD, Panic Disorder, and even depression with anxious features can be helped with anti-anxiety drugs.

Antidepressants

These medicines are used for a variety of psychiatric disorders and can be very effective in treating depression for adults and children. While antidepressants may cause a wide range of side effects, these medications are usually well tolerated under proper care. Interestingly, antidepressants are also useful for anxiety diagnoses such as OCD, Generalized Anxiety Disorder, Panic Disorder, and even bulimia.

Mood Stabilizers

This class of medicine is commonly used with adults and is increasingly prescribed in child and adolescent psychiatry, as disorders of mood have become a common diagnosis. Bipolar disorder is now seen as moderately common, and the spectrum of that disorder—mood irritability and instability—appears to respond to these medicines.

Antipsychotics

These potent medicines sound daunting, but they can be effective in common psychiatric problems, such as Pervasive Developmental Disorder, mood disorders, and even for the management of aggression. As a class, antipsychotics were designed for people who have lost touch with reality, but in lower doses they can be a great help to some children and teenagers. These medicines are often used off-label, so it is important to carefully question your doctor before she prescribes it. Ask about side effects that can be problematic.

Common Sleep Agents

Problems falling and staying asleep stem from a variety of sources and require treatments that are targeted to a specific cause. Treatments range from anxiolytics to mood stabilizers and antidepressants. Occasional use of an antihistamine or melatonin may help as long as it is given under a doctor's supervision. Commonly used sleep aids should be used very cautiously.

Glossary

Abuse: To use or treat wrongly or badly, especially in a way that is to your own advantage; to use rude or cruel language; the wrong use of privilege, power, or someone's kindness; the treatment of children in a bad way— verbally, physically, or sexually.

Adjustment Disorder: The inability to adapt to stress manifesting in an emotional or behavioral disorder.

Attention Deficit Hyperactivity Disorder (ADHD): A neurobehavioral disorder often characterized by an inability to concentrate or listen as well as a lack of organization.

Binuclear family: An extended family consisting of two households; usually comprised of children and the subsequent spouses of partners in a divorce.

Bipolar Disorder: A psychiatric disorder often characterized by severe mood swings between a manic and depressive state.

Child and adolescent psychiatrists: Physicians who have been trained in child development and can provide assessment, therapy, and medications if required.

Child and adolescent psychologists: Academic professionals trained to assess and treat a child's learning issues and/or psychological problems that may be present.

Coparenting: Parents work as a team although they are no longer together.

Counseling: Professional help with problems of a personal or psychological nature.

Depression: A medical illness characterized by persistent sadness.

Displacement: A defense mechanism in which emotions from one issue are refocused onto another less threatening person or object.

DSM IV: *Diagnostic and Statistical Manual of Mental Disorders*: a reference guide utilized by mental health professionals in the diagnosis of psychological disorders.

Dysthymia: Mild, chronic depression.

Eating Disorder: Irregular or detrimental eating habits resulting in dysfunction. Two predominant eating disorders are anorexia and bulimia; the former is expressed through a very strict intake of food and the latter is identified by bingeing and purging.

Empathy: Comprehension of another person's feelings/emotions.

Intergenerational Boundary: The division between the world of adults and the world of their children.

Learning Disorders: A brain disorder in which an individual has difficulty understanding, processing, remembering, or responding to new information.

Major Depressive Disorder: A serious form of depression.

Mediation: Intervention for the sake of amicably resolving a conflict.

Mirroring: Emulating someone else while communicating with them.

Obsessive Compulsive Disorder (OCD): Anxiety disorder often characterized by repetitive thoughts and behaviors.

Parental abduction: Circumstances in which the child is taken by one parent for a period of time without the consent or knowledge of the other parent.

Personality Disorder: Mental illness that debilitates an individual's thinking, perception, and relationships with others, making real social reciprocity impossible.

Physical abuse: The use of physical force to intentionally cause harm to another person.

Psychotherapist: A mental health professional utilizing communication of feelings and thoughts, in order to ameliorate psychological distress in an individual.

Psychotherapy: Process in which psychological problems are treated via communication and relationship factors between an individual and a therapist.

Psychotic thinking: Thought processes that are out of touch with reality.

Regression: Psychological term describing how people under stress "regress" to an earlier state of functioning.

Repetition Compulsion: A phenomenon in which a person will reenact circumstances of a traumatic event; the reenactment of emotional experiences.

Self-preservation: The instinctive behavior to defend oneself from harm.

Sexual abuse: Any sexual activity performed on a child whether it is fondling, genital touching or penetration.

Triangulation: A parent's use of alliances with a child in order to undermine the other parent.

Verbal abuse: The use of words in the form of criticism and insults to intentionally cause harm to another individual.

References

Afifi, T. O., Cox, B. J., and Enns, M. W. (2006). Mental health profiles among married, never-married, and separated/ divorced mothers in a nationally representative sample. *Social Psychiatry and Psychiatric Epidemiology, 41*(2), 122–129. doi: 10.1007/s00127-005-0005-3.

Ahrons, C. (2004). *We're still family: What grown children have to say about their parents' divorce.* New York, NY: HarperCollins.

Ahrons, C. (1994). *The good divorce: Keeping your family together when your marriage comes apart.* New York: HarperCollins.

Amato, P. R., & Keith, B. (1991). Parental divorce and the well-being of children: A meta-analysis. *Psychological Bulletin, 110*(1), 26–46. doi:10.1037/0033-2909.110.1.26

American Academy of Child and Adolescent Psychiatry (2009). *Child and Adolescent Mental Illness and Drug Abuse Statistics.* www.aacap.org/cs/root/resources_for_families/ child_and_adolescent_mental_illness_statistics.

American Academy of Pediatrics (1999). *Child Abuse and Neglect. www.medem.com/?q=medlib/article/ ZZZ3S3DRUDC.*

Banschick, M. R., & Silman, J. (2003). Children in cyberspace. In L. Shyles, *Deciphering cyberspace: Making the most of digital communication technology.* Thousand Oaks, CA: Sage Publications.

Baum, N. (2004). On helping divorced men to mourn their losses. *American Journal of Psychotherapy, 58*(2), 174–185.

Baum, N. (2003). The male way of mourning divorce: When, what, and how. *Clinical Social Work Journal, 31*(1), 37–50. doi: 10.1023/A:1021462517875

Beck, A. T. (1976). *Cognitive therapy and the emotional disorders.* New York, NY: Meridian.

Bennett, M. P., Zeller, J. M., Rosenberg, L. & McCann, J. (2003). The effect of mirthful laughter on stress and natural killer cell activity. *Alternative Therapies in Health and Medicine, 9*(2), 38–43.

Benson, H. (1999). "Belief Can Induce Healing by Evoking the Relaxation Response." in *Healing Through Prayer* Edited by Larry Dossey. Anglican Book Centre.

Bernardo, M. R. (Interviewer), & Morrison, S. (Interviewee). (2010, March 30). The key to surviving divorce – by 'Redbook' editor Stacy Morrison [Web log comment]. *lemondrop.* Retrieved from http://www.lemondrop.com/2010/03/30/how-to-survive-a-divorce-stacy-morrison-redbook/

Bisnaire, et al. (1990). *Factors Associated with Academic Achievement in Children Following Parental Separation.* American Journal of Orthopsychiatry.

Bowen, M. (1990). *Family Therapy in Clinical Practice.* New York: Jason Aronson.

Bradshaw, M., Ellison, C. G., & Flannelly, K. J. (2008). Prayer, god imagery, and symptoms of psychopathology. *Journal for the Scientific Study of Religion, 47*(4), 644–659. doi:10.1111/j.1468-5906.2008.00432.x

Bruce, M. L., & Kim, K. M. (1992). Differences in the effects of divorce on Major Depression in men and women. *The American Journal of Psychiatry, 149*(7), 914–917.

Burns, D. D. (2009). *Feeling good: The new mood therapy.* New York, NY: Harper.

Centers for Disease Control and Prevention (2007a). Health benefits of pets. Retrieved from http://www.cdc.gov/healthypets/health_benefits.htm

Centers for Disease Control and Prevention (2007b). Sleep and chronic disease. Retrieved from: http://www.cdc.gov/sleep/chronic_disease.htm

Centers for Disease Control and Prevention & National Center for Injury Prevention and Control (2009). *Understanding child maltreatment: Factsheet.* Retrieved January 9, 2010, from http://www.cdc.gov/violenceprevention/pdf/CM-FactSheet-a.pdf

Clark, D. A., Beck, A. T. & Alford, B. A. (1999). *Scientific foundations of cognitive theory and therapy of depression.* New York, NY: John Wiley & Sons.

Cook, J. (Compiler & Arranger). (1999). *The Book of Positive Quotations.* New York, N.Y.

Cooper, A. *Cybersex: The Dark Side of the Force.* Al Cooper. Brunner-Routledge, 2000

Covey, S. R. (1990). *The 7 habits of highly effective people: Powerful lessons in personal change.* New York, NY: Fireside.

Curtner-Smith, M. and MacKinnon-Lewis. (1994). *Family Process Effects on Adolescent Males' Susceptibility to Antisocial Peer Pressure.* Journal of Family Relations.

Dawson, D.A. (1991). *Family structure and children's health: data from the 1988 National Survey of Child Health.* Journal of Marriage and the Family.

Diagnostic and Statistical Manual for Mental Disorders – DSM IV. (1994). American Psychiatric Association

Fraiberg, S. (1956). *The magic years: Understanding and handling the problems of early childhood.* New York: Scribner.

Frazier, P., Steward, J., & Mortensen, H. (2004). Perceived control and adjustment to trauma: A comparison across events. *Journal of Social and Clinical Psychology, 23*(3), 303–324. doi:10.1521/jscp.23.3.303.35452

Frewen, P. A., Evans, E. M., Maraj, N., Dozois, D. J. A., & Partridge, K. (2008). Letting go: Mindfulness and negative automatic thinking. *Cognitive Therapy and Research, 32*(6), 758–774. doi:10.1007/s10608-007-9142-1

Fromm, E. (1950). *Psychoanalysis and Religion.* New York: Yale University Press.

Frost, R. (2006). Mending wall. In D. Lehman (Ed.), *The Oxford book of American poetry* (pp. 212–13). New York, NY: Oxford. (Original work published 1914).

Gabbard, G. O. (2009). *Textbook of psychotherapeutic treatments.* Washington, DC: American Psychiatric Publishing.

Garasky, S. (1995). *The Effects of Family Structure on Educational Attainment: Do the Effects Vary by the Age of the Child?* American Journal of Economics and Sociology.

Green, W. (2006). *Child and Adolescent Clinical Psychopharmacology.* New York: Lippincott.

Greenspan, S (1999*). Building Healthy Minds.* Perseus Publishing.

Greenspan, S. (1997). *The Growth of the Mind.* Da Capo Press.

Hammer, H., Finkelhor, D., & Sedlak, A. J. (2002). Children abducted by family members: National estimates and characteristics (NCJ 196466). Retrieved from http://www.ncjrs.gov/pdffiles1/ojjdp/196466.pdf

Hefner, J. & Eisenberg, D. (2009). Social support and mental health among college students. *American Journal of Orthopsychiatry, 79*(4), 491–499. doi:10.1037/a0016918

Hendrix, H. Getting The Love You Want: A Guide For Couples, 1988

Herring, M. P., O'Conner, P. J., & Dishman, R. K. (2010). The effect of exercise training on anxiety symptoms among patients: A systematic review. *Archives of Internal Medicine, 170*(4), 321–331.

Hertherington, E. M. (2002*). For Better or For Worse Divorce Reconsidered.* New York: W.W. Norton & Co., 2002.

Hyman, M. (2007). The first mind-body medicine: Bringing Shamanism into the 21st century. *Alternative Therapies in Health and Medicine, 13*(4), 10–11.

Jonas, W. B., & Crawford, C. C. (2003). Science and spiritual healing: a critical review of spiritual healing, "energy" medicine, and intentionality. *Alternative Therapies in Health and Medicine, 9*(2), 56–61.

Karlter, N. (1935). *Implications of parental divorce for female development.* Journal of the American Academy of Child Psychiatry.

Kaufman, M. (2004, June 23). Cigarettes cut about 10 years off life, 50-year study shows: British survey of smoking doctors details long-term risks. *The Washington Post.* Retrieved from http://www.washingtonpost.com/wp-dyn/articles/A61981-2004Jun22.html

Kershaw, S. (2009). "Marijuana Is Gateway Drug for Two Debates." *N.Y. Times.* www.nytimes.com/2009/07/19/fashion/19pot.html?_r=1&emc=eta1.

Kiecolt-Glaser, J. K., McGuire, L., Robles, T. F., & Glaser, R. (2002). Emotions, morbidity, and mortality: New perspectives from psychoneuroimmunology. *Annual Review of Psychology, 53*(1), 83-107. doi:10.1146/annurev.psych.53.100901.135217

Kposowa, A. J. (2000). Marital status and suicide in the National Longitudinal Mortality Study. *Journal of Epidemiology & Community Health, 54*(4), 254–261. doi:10.1136/jech.54.4.254

Kübler-Ross, E., and Kessler, D. (n.d.). The Five Stages of Grief. Retrieved from http://grief.com/the-five-stages-of-grief/

Kushner, M. A. (2009). A review of the empirical literature about child development and adjustment post-separation. *Journal of Divorce and Remarriage, 50,* 496–516.

Larson, D. B., Swyers, J. P., & Larson, S. S. The costly consequences of divorce: Assessing the clinical, economic, and public health impact of marital disruption in the United States. A research-based seminar." Rockville, Maryland: National Institute for Healthcare Research.

Lorenz, F. O., Wickrama, K. A. S., Conger, R. D., & Elder, G. H. (2006). The short-term and decade-long effects of divorce on women's midlife health. *Journal of Health and Social Behavior, 47*(2), 111–125. doi:10.1177/002214650604700202

Maltby, J., Lewis, C. A., & Day, L. (2008). Prayer and subjective well-being: The application of a cognitive-behavioural framework. *Mental Health, Religion & Culture, 11*(1), 119–129. doi:10.1080/13674670701485722

Mesa Community College Psychology Department. *(1997). Correlation between Divorce and Child Sexual Abuse. www.mc.maricopa.edu/dept/d46/psy/dev/Spring01/Divorce/abuse.html*

Manzoni, G. M., Pagnini, F., Castelnuovo, G., & Molinari, E. (2008).Relaxation training for anxiety: A ten-years systematic review with meta-analysis. *BMC Psychiatry, 8*(41). doi: 10.1186/1471-244X-8-41

McCullough, M. E., Hoyt, W. T., Larson, D. B., Koenig, H. G., & Thoresen, C. (2000). Religious involvement and mortality:

A meta-analytic review. *Health Psychology, 19*(3), 211–222. doi:10.1037/0278-6133.19.3.211

Mittleman, M. A. (2000). Marital stress worsens prognosis in women with coronary heart disease: The Stockholm female coronary risk study. *Journal of the American Medical Association, 284*(23), 3008–3014. doi:10.1001/jama.284.23.3008

Morrison, S. (2010). *Falling apart in one piece: One optimist's journey through the hell of divorce.* New York, NY: Simon & Schuster.

National Center for Health Statistics (1970). *Mortality from selected causes by marital status* (Public Health Service Publication No. 1000-Series 20-No. 8). Washington, DC: U.S. Government Printing Office. Retrieved from http://www.cdc.gov/nchs/data/series/sr_20/sr20_008aacc.pdf (Part A) & http://www.cdc.gov/nchs/data/series/sr_20/sr20_008bacc.pdf (Park B)

National Institutes of Health (2006). In brief: Your guide to healthy sleep (NIH Publication No. 06–5800). Retrieved from http://www.nhlbi.nih.gov/health/public/sleep/healthysleepfs.pdf

National Institute on Drug Abuse. (2008). *NIDA InfoFacts: High School and Youth Trends. www.drugabuse.gov/infofacts/HSYouthTrends.html*

National Institute of Mental Health (2009). *Statistics.* Retrieved from http://www.nimh.nih.gov/health/topics/statistics/index.shtml

National Institute of Neurological Disorders and Stroke (2007). Brain basics: Understanding sleep (NIH Publication No.06-3440-c). Retrieved from *http://www.ninds.nih.gov/disorders/brain_basics/understanding_sleep.htm*

Nicholson, A., Rose, R., & Bobak, M. (2010). Associations between different dimensions of religious involvement and self-rated health in diverse European populations. *Health Psychology, 29*(2), 227–235. doi:10.1037/a0018036

Nilsson, P.M., Nilsson, J. –A., Hedblad, B., & Berglund, G. (2001). Sleep disturbance in associated with elevated pulse rate for prediction of mortality—consequences of mental strain? *Journal of Internal Medicine, 250*(6). 521–529.

NIMH. (2008). *The Numbers Count: Mental Disorders in America.* ww.nimh.nih.gov/health/publications/the-numbers-count-mental-disordersnamerica/index.shtml#Intro

O'Neill, E. (2002). *Long day's journey into night* (2nd Ed.). New Haven, CT: Yale Nota Bene.

Orth-Gomér, K., Wamala, S. P., Horsten, M., Schenck-Gustafsson, K., Schneiderman, N. &

Park, S., & Mattson, R. H. (2009). Ornamental indoor plants in hospital rooms enhanced health outcomes of patients recovering from surgery. *The Journal of Alternative and Complimentary Medicine, 15*(9), 975–980. doi:10.1089=acm.2009.0075

Parker-Pope, T. (2010, April 12). Is marriage good for your health? *New York Times Magazine.* Retrieved from *http://www.nytimes.com/2010/04/18/magazine/18marriage-t.html*

Pesta, A. (Interviewer), & Obama, M. (Interviewee). Michelle Obama keeps it real. *marie claire.* Retrieved from http://www.marieclaire.com/world-reports/news/latest/michelle-obama-interview-media

Pine, F. (1985). *Developmental Theory and Clinical Process.* New York: Basic Books.

Scheier, M. F., & Carver, C. S. (1993). On the power of positive thinking: The benefits of being optimistic.

Current Directions in Psychological Science, 2(1), 26–30. doi: 10.1111/1467-8721.ep10770572

Schmidt, S., & Walach, H. (2004) Mindfulness-based stress reduction and health benefits: A meta-analysis. *Journal of Psychosomatic Research, 57*(1), 35–43. doi:10.1016/S0022-3999(03)00573-7

Schoenborn, C.A., & Adams, P.F. (2010). Health behaviors of adults: United States, 2005–2007 (DHHS Publication No. [PHS] 2010–1573). Washington, DC: U.S. Government Printing Office.

Schoenborn, C.A. (2004). Marital status and health: United States, 1999–2002 (DHHS Publication No. [PHS] 2005-1250 05-0034 [12/04]). Hyattsville, MD.

Serenity Prayer (n.d). Retrieved from http://www. thevoiceforlove.com/serenity-prayer.html

Solomon, A. (2003). Noonday demon. New York, NY: Scribner.

Steinberg, L.D. (1987). *Single parents, stepparents, and the susceptibility of adolescents to antisocial peer pressure.* Journal of Child Development.

Stewart, R. E., & Chambless, D. L. (2009). Cognitive–behavioral therapy for adult anxiety disorders in clinical practice: A meta-analysis of effectiveness studies. *Journal of Consulting and Clinical Psychology, 77*(4), 595–606. doi:10.1037/a0016032

Stowell, J. R., Kiecolt-Glaser, J. K., & Glaser, R. (2001). Perceived stress and cellular immunity: When coping counts. *Journal of Behavioral Medicine, 24*(4), 323–339. doi:10.1023/A:1010630801589

Thoreau, H. D. (1995). *Walden: Or, life in the woods.* Mineola, NY: Dover Publications

Uchino, B. N., Cacioppo, J. T., & Kiecolt-Glaser, J. K. (1996). The relationship between social support and physiological processes: A review with emphasis on underlying mechanisms and implications for health. *Psychological Bulletin, 119*(3), 488–531. doi: 10.1037/0033-2909.119.3.488

U. S. Center for Disease Control. (2008). "Births, Marriages, Divorces, and Deaths: Provisional Data for 2007." *National Vital Statistic Reports.* Vol. 56 No. 21.

U. S. Department of Justice. *ABC's of legal terms.* Retrieved January 9, 2010, from the United States Attorneys Kids Page, Inside the Courtroom Web site: *http://www.justice. gov/usao/eousa/kidspage/glossary.html*

U. S. Department of Justice. (2002). Highlights from the NISMART bulletins. Retrieved from http://www.ncjrs. gov/html/ojjdp/nismart/05/index.html

Vimmerstedt, S., & Mercer, J. I wanna be around. Retrieved from http://www.lyricsdepot.com/tony-bennett/i-wanna-be-around.html

Wallerstein, J. (2000). *The Unexpected Legacy of Divorce.* New York: Hyperion.

Wallerstein, J. S., and Kelly, J. B. (1998). *Surviving the breakup: How children and parents cope with divorce.* New York: Basic Books

Wenk-Sormaz, H. (2005). Meditation can reduce habitual responding. *Alternative Therapies in Health and Medicine, 2*(2), 42–58.

Zhang, Z., & Hayward, M. D. (2006). Gender, the marital life course, and cardiovascular disease in late midlife. *Journal of Marriage and Family, 68*(3), 639–657. doi:10.1111/j.1741-3737.2006.00280.x

Index

Debt, 239, 241, 243–4
Deceit, 58
Deferred Compensation, 250–1
Denial, 54–5, 58, 60
Dependent, 47, 259–60. *See also* Dependent Personality Disorder.
Dependent Personality Disorder, 309–10
Depression, 23, 58–9, 61–2, 75–7, 152, 170, 179, 216, 219–21, 257–8, 264
Detoxing, 163–5, 178
Developmental milestones, 211–5
Diagnostic and Statistical Manual of Mental Disorders DSM IV, 318
Digestive problems, 169
Dinner, 165, 167–8
Disability, 63, 303
Disabling anger. *See* Red Brain Anger.
Disabling anxiety. *See* Gray Brain.
Disappointment, 55, 59, 104, 129
Displacement, 34–5, 146, 318
DivorceCare, 202
Doctor, 23, 61, 76, 138, 154, 170–1, 173–4, 177, 222, 260–2, 266, 313–5
Drug Counselors, 155
Drugs, abuse of, 79–82, 131, 155, 199, 217–8, 257, 264, 300, 308–9. *See also* Pharmaceuticals.
Dysfunction, 77, 131, 307. *See also particular kinds of dysfunction.*
Dysthymia (dysthymic disorder), 220, 257, 301, 318

E
Eating Disorders, 301, 318
Effective Communication, 19–21
Effectiveness, 195
Elliptical machine, 175
Emotionally unstable, 67, 308, 314
Emotions and Food, 169–71

Empathy, 318
Endorphins, 175
Energy, 59, 131, 191
  agitated, 135, 139
  lack of, 58, 61, 75, 230
  manic, 220, 300
  nutrition and, 166
Environmental Protection Agency (EPA), 161
Equitable distribution, 241–2
Equity, 241, 251
Erikson, Erik, 224
Estate, 239–43, 246–7, 249, 251
Estrogen, 258
Ethical Cultural, 201
Everything Starts from Prayer, 197
Exercise, 23, 135, 139, 148, 153, 171, 173–8, 180. *See also Fitness.*
Existential analysis, 151–2
Expectations, 175

F
Facebook, 203
Fatigue, 129, 150, 193
Fear, 9, 24, 74, 150, 237, 302–3
Feelings-based approach, 129, 151–2
Fellini, Federico, 136
Fiber, 164, 166
Financial planners, 240, 249–50, 252
Financial Primer, 237–52
Fish, 161
Fitness, 23, 135, 139, 148, 153, 171, 173–8, 180
Flexibility training, 176, 178
Florida, state of, 91
Food, 67, 153, 159–73
Food and Drug Administration (FDA), 161, 313
Forensic accountant, 240, 244
Freedom, 83–4
Freud, Sigmund, 58, 70, 101

Acknowledgments

This book is a labor of love, dedicated to my mother, Helen Banschick, and my father, Sheren Banschick. Each gave me the love and wisdom to live a balanced life (or at least try) and pursue what makes me happy. I still have the pleasure of thanking my mother in person, but as for my father, I can only hope that he is smiling in the next world.

Once again, I am very pleased to acknowledge my wife, Josefa Silman, M.Ed., who was the primary researcher and co-author of the original *The Intelligent Divorce* course. She has been an enthusiastic supporter, my great friend, and partner. And while speaking about my family, I couldn't imagine a better set of wonderful children: Gabriel, Micah and Chaya. Whenever I need some good energy, I know where to turn.

I would like to acknowledge the contributions of the following colleagues and friends:

Peter Acker, M.D., believed in the *Intelligent Divorce* project and offered me an opportunity to present this work at Greenwich Hospital, which became an impetus to spread the word to the medical community.

Kevin Kalikow, M.D., is a child psychiatrist, colleague and dear friend, who added his fair share to this book. Our bi-weekly lunches have been a staple for the past fifteen years, which is really impressive when you think about it.

Deborah Karel, M.A., is a psychotherapist extraordinaire who co-taught the original divorce course which was crucial in developing a rough product from theory to practice. Her ability to share her own experience deepened what the course has done for its participants.

Micki McWade, M.S.W., is the insightful author of *Getting Up, Getting Over, Getting On*. Her spiritual, twelve-step approach to divorce has made Micki a natural partner. Her enthusiasm and pragmatism are both embedded in this book.

Coryn Rosenstock worked on this second book as an intern before entering law school. She made a tremendous contribution with her amazing research skills and love of writing. The legal profession is lucky to have her.

Jonah Schrag, Psy.D, is a therapist and mediator of the highest quality. I trust him with everything that is important. Thanks for your insight about mediation, collaborative law, and divorce, in general.

Leonard Shyles, Ph.D., is someone who I have known for more years than I can count. Thank you for your encouragement and love. Len, you are a lot of fun and, for better or worse, you got me started on this road of writing books.

For their insight and support, I'd like to thank Elie Abemayor, M.D., Jill Brooke, Richard Francis, M.D. the late Nancy Gardner, M.S.W., John Gerson, Ph.D., Deborah Gershon, M.S.W., Louis Getoff, Ph.D., Ariela Goldstein, M.S.W., James Hollis, Ph.D., Sam Klagsbrun, M.D., Dan Lobel, Ph.D., Jeffrey Rubin, Ph.D., Carol Ochs, Ph.D., Lawrence Horowitz, Esq., Sue Collier, Cindy Blum, M.S., C.H.T., P.L.R.T., Louis Corsaro, M.D., Rabbi Rueven Flamer, Rabbi Eli Krimsky, Stuart Silverstein, M.D., Roberta Stiel, Psy.D., Ronnie Falkenberg, M.A., Margaret Clark, Esq., Anne Winnestrand, M.S.W., Kelly Donovan, Esq., Guita Sazan, Ph.D.,

Allison Bell, Psy.D., Jackie Schiff, Ph.D., Dan Fried, Linda Liotti, and Michael Stromes, M.Ed.

A special thanks to Geri Brewster, R.D., M.P.H., C.D.N., Pamela Tinkham, M.S.W., Rory Pinto, C.B.H.S., and Victor Grossman, Esq., who helped craft the chapters on nutrition, fitness, meditation, and law. Their insights were invaluable.

I would also like to acknowledge the work of my production team: Michele DeFilippo, Ronda Rawlins, and their colleagues at 1106 Design, as well as Cathi Stevenson and Jana Guothova, for their work on the cover, and Edna Cabcabin Moran for the book's wonderful illustrations. When speaking about production, I can't leave out The Nerdy Duo, Melissa Weiland and Erin Cardullo, for their video production work, and Joshua Gershman and Edan Dover for great websites that blend video and prose so beautifully. I'd also like to thank attorneys Bernice Kosowsky, Esq., and Carl Durham, Esq. as well as my research assistants, Mikko Harvey, Hanna Warman, Devin Schiff, Chelsea Slosberg, Leann Longi, and Tim Pasternack. These individuals hail from around the globe, including Phoenix, San Francisco, Los Angeles, Denver, New York, Halifax, and even Slovakia.

Last, but certainly not least is David Tabatsky, M.A., V.D.D. (Veteran of a Difficult Divorce), who is my collaborator and friend. David contributed significantly to this book and edited even more. Most important, he made me think. And even better, he made me laugh.

Thank you all!

Mark R. Banschick, M.D.

About the Authors

Mark R. Banschick is a member of the American Psychiatric Association and the American Academy of Child and Adolescent Psychiatry and is a Diplomate of the American Board of Psychiatry and Neurology.

He received a Bachelor of Arts from Vassar College and a Doctorate in Medicine from Sackler Medical School in Tel Aviv, Israel. After a residency in general psychiatry at Georgetown University Hospital, he did a fellowship in child and adolescent psychiatry at the Cornell Medical Center in New York. Dr. Banschick also completed a program in religious studies at the PARDES Institute for Jewish Studies in Jerusalem.

At the renowned Four Winds Hospital in Westchester, New York, Dr. Banschick served as a unit chief for the Psychiatric Transition Service and as Director of the Child Outpatient Service. He has served as an expert witness for custody disputes for many years and designed and taught The Intelligent Divorce since 1998.

Dr. Banschick is the author of *The Intelligent Divorce,* including *Book One: Taking Care of Your Children (2010).* He has contributed chapters on child development and the spirituality of young people in *Deciphering Cyberspace* (Sage Publications, 2003), *The Power of Prayer* (New World Library, 1998), and *The Handbook of Child Psychiatry* (Wiley, 1997), among others.

He has appeared on CBS's *The Early Show,* as well as *The New York Times, The Huffington Post* and FirstWivesWorld.com.

Dr. Banschick currently teaches in the doctoral program at Hebrew Union College in New York City.

His private practice is located in Katonah, New York.

Dr. Banschick lives with his wife, Josefa, and has three children: Gabe, Micah, and Chaya.

David Tabatsky is a writer, editor, teacher, director, and performing artist. He received his B.A. in Communications and an M.A. in Theatre Education, both from Adelphi University in Garden City, New York.

David is the coauthor of *The Intelligent Divorce* book series. He is the coauthor of *The Cancer Book: 101 Stories of Courage, Support and Love*, from the Chicken Soup for the Soul series (2009). He is the coauthor with Randy Wright, M.D., of *The Wright Choice: Your Family Prescription for Healthy Eating, Modern Fitness, & Saving Money* (2011). He is the coauthor, with Bruce Kluger, of *Dear President Obama: Letters of Hope From Children Across America* (2009). David wrote *The Boy Behind the Door: How Salomon Kool Escaped the Nazis* (2009).

He was the Consulting Editor for Marlo Thomas and her New York Times bestseller *The Right Words at the Right Time, Volume 2: Your Turn!* (2006).

David has published two editions of *What's Cool Berlin*, a comic travel guide to Germany's capital, and has written for *The Forward*, *Parenting*, and *Sesame Street Parent*, among others.

David has worked professionally in theatre and circus as an actor, clown, and juggler, appearing in New York at Lincoln Center, Radio City Music Hall, the Beacon Theatre and throughout the United States, Europe, Russia, and Japan, including his critically acclaimed solo performance at the Edinburgh Fringe Festival. He played a significant role in the resurgence of the *Variete* movement in Germany, with original shows at the *Chamaleon* in Berlin and the *Schmidt* in Hamburg, among others. He also directed *Kinderzirkus Taborka* at the renowned Tempodrom in Berlin.

David has taught for the American School of London, die Etage in Berlin, the Big Apple Circus School, the United Nations International School, and The Cathedral of St. John the Divine. He serves on the theatre faculty at Adelphi University and is a teaching artist for The Henry Street Settlement with a focus on special education.

David is divorced and lives in New York City with his children, Max and Stella.

Please visit www.tabatsky.com.

Family Stabilization Course For Busy Parents

In addition to our *Intelligent Divorce* book series, we offer a very reasonably-priced online parenting course, and you will receive a certificate upon completion. You may find it helpful for you and your children.

Please visit: *www.FamilyStabilizationCourse.com* for more details.

Note: Many courts in the United States and Canada require parenting classes during divorce. While our Family Stabilization Course is designed to help parents, whether mandated or not, the course has been created with the court system in mind — if they accept an on-line format. Check with your attorney or judge to find out if our course is appropriate for your individual legal situation.

Intelligent Book Press

The Intelligent Divorce
Because Your Kids Come First
Available from Intelligent Book Press

Book One
(2010)
Taking Care of Your Children

Book Two
(2011)
Taking Care of Yourself

Book Three
(2012)
Dealing With Your (Impossible) Ex

For more information please visit
www.theintelligentdivorce.com

Order Form

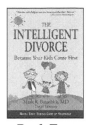

Book One
Taking Care of Your Children

Book Two
Taking Care of Yourself
(So Your Kids Don't Have To)

By mail:
  Intelligent Book Press
  c/o Port City Fufillment Services
  35 Ash Drive
  Kimball, MI 48074 USA

By internet:
  www.theintelligentdivorce.com

By phone:
  1-888-99-MYFAMILY or 1-888-996-9 3 2 6 (ILY)

Quantity	Book Title	Each	Total
	Taking Care of Your Children	$15.95	
	Taking Care of Yourself	$19.95	
	SUBTOTAL		
	Shipping and Handling **USA:** Shipping 5.95 + 1.00 Each Additional Book Free Shipping over 5 books **Canada:** Shipping 9.95 + 2.00 Each Additional Book Free Shipping over 5 books **Europe:** Shipping 14.95 + 4.00 Each Additional Book Free Shipping over 10 books		
	TOTAL		

Ship to: (Please use credit card statement address)

Name: _____

Address: _____

City, State, Zip: _____

Phone: _____Email (optional): _____

Payment method:

☐ Check/Money Order (payable to "Port City Fufillment Services" in US$ and drawn on a US Bank)

☐ Visa   ☐ Mastercard   ☐ AMEX (Statement will reflect a charge to "Port City Fufillment Services")

Card No: _____

Exp. date: _____/_____Card Security Code _____ (Required)

Cardholder name (Print): _____

Card Signature: _____

> *"If I am not for myself, who will be there for me?*
> *If I am only for myself, what am I?*
> *If not now, when?"*
>
> Hillel, First Century A.D.

306.89

15004046R00195

Made in the USA
Lexington, KY
05 May 2012